PIANO / VOCAL / GUITAR

MARIAH THE BALLADS

T0069473

ISBN 978-1-4234-7451-7

HAL•LEONARD®
CORPORATION

7777 W. BLUEMOUND RD. P.O. BOX 13819 MILWAUKEE, WI 53213

Visit Hal Leonard Online at
www.halleonard.com

ALWAYS BE MY BABY

Words and Music by MARIAH CAREY,
JERMAINE DUPRI and MANUEL SEAL

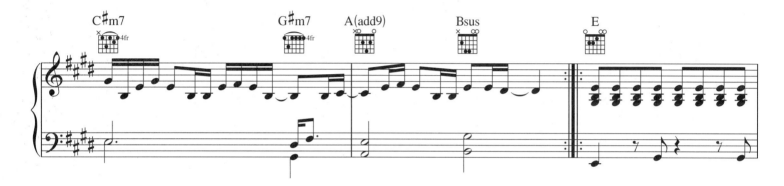

We were as one, babe, for a mo-ment in time.

I ain't gon-na cry, no, and I won't beg you to stay.

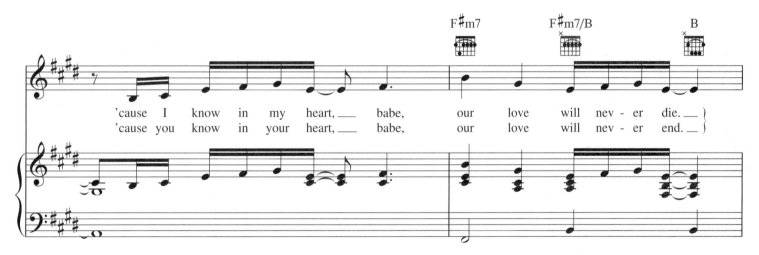

Boy, don't you know you can't es - cape __ me. Ooh, dar - ling, 'cause you'll al - ways be __ my ba -

- by. And we'll lin - ger on. __ Time can't e - rase a feel - ing this strong. __

No way you're ev - er gon - na shake __ me. Ooh, dar - ling, 'cause you'll al - ways be __ my ba -

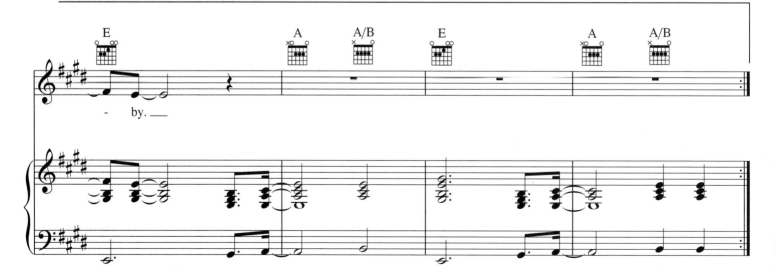

- by. __

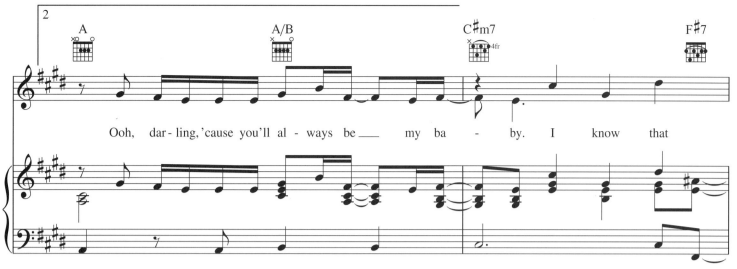

Ooh, dar-ling, 'cause you'll al-ways be ___ my ba - by. I know that

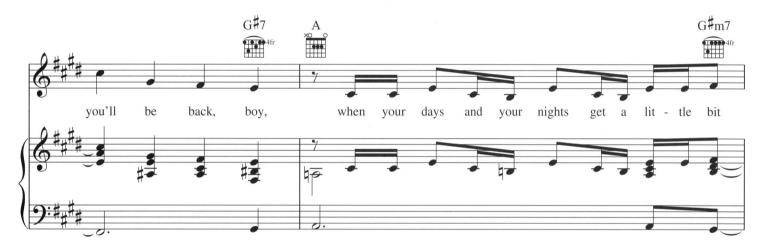

you'll be back, boy, when your days and your nights get a lit-tle bit

cold - er. ___ I know that you'll be right back, ba - by.

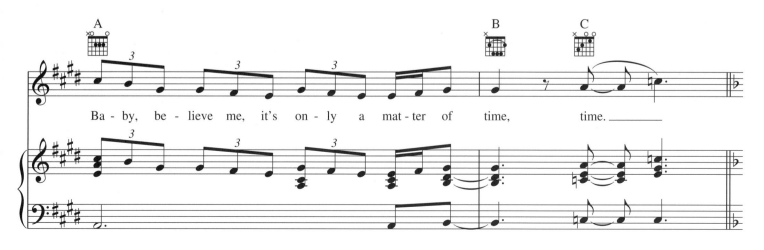

Ba - by, be - lieve me, it's on - ly a mat-ter of time, time. ___

You'll al-ways be a part of me. ___ I'm part of you in-def-i-nite-ly. _____
-by.

Boy, don't you know you can't es-cape ___ me. Ooh, dar-ling,'cause you'll al-ways be ___ my ba-

-by. And we'll lin-ger on. ___ Time can't e-rase a feel-ing this strong. ___

Repeat and Fade

No way you're ev-er gon-na shake ___ me. Oh, dar-ling,'cause you'll al-ways be ___ my ba-

DREAMLOVER

Words and Music by MARIAH CAREY,
DAVID PORTER and DAVE HALL

Moderately

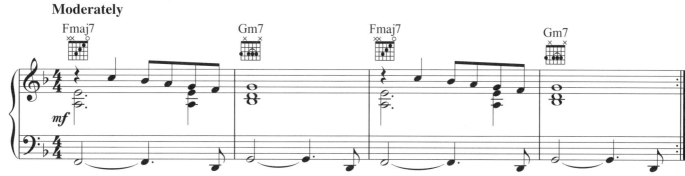

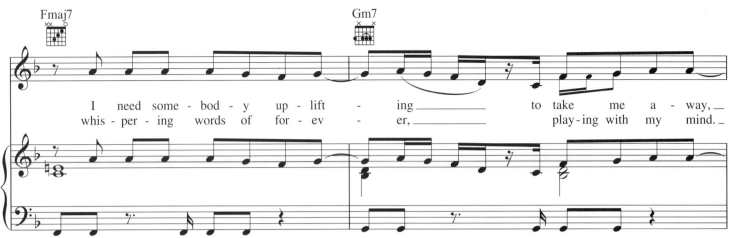

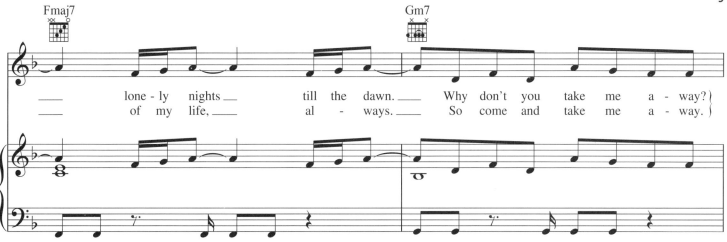

lone - ly nights ___ till the dawn. ___ Why don't you take me a - way?
of my life, ___ al - ways. ___ So come and take me a - way.

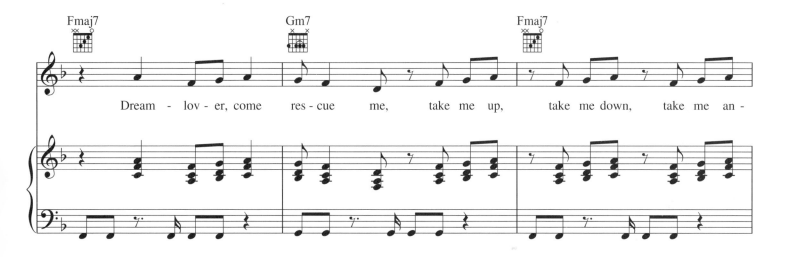

Dream - lov - er, come res - cue me, take me up, take me down, take me an -

y - where you want to, ba - by, now. I need you so des - p'rate - ly. Won't you please

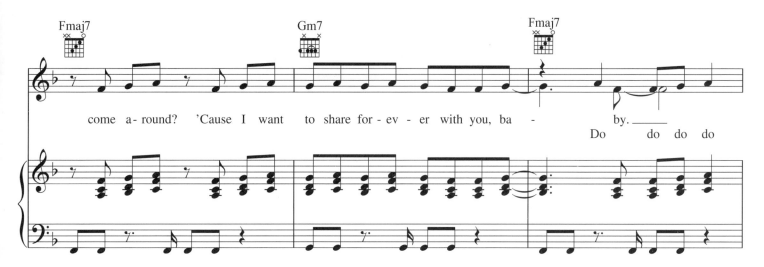

come a - round? 'Cause I want to share for - ev - er with you, ba - by. ___
Do do do do

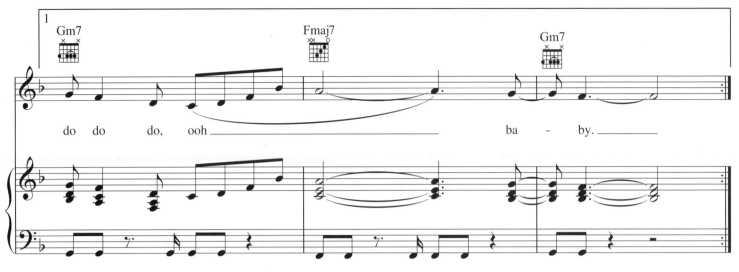

do do do, ooh _____ ba - by. _____

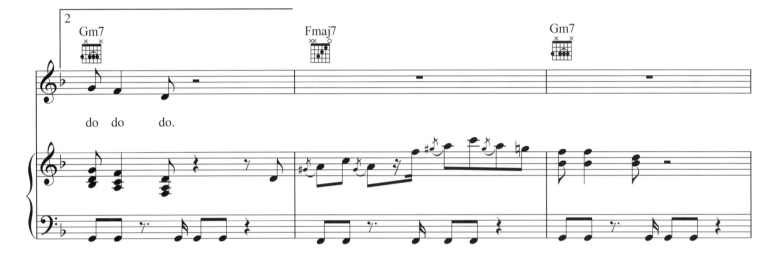

do do do.

Do do do do do do do. Do do do do

do do do. Dream - lov - er, come res - cue me, take me up,

take me down, take me an - y - where you want to, ba - by, now. I need you so

des p'rate - ly. Won't you please come a - round? 'Cause I want to share for - ev - er with you, ba -

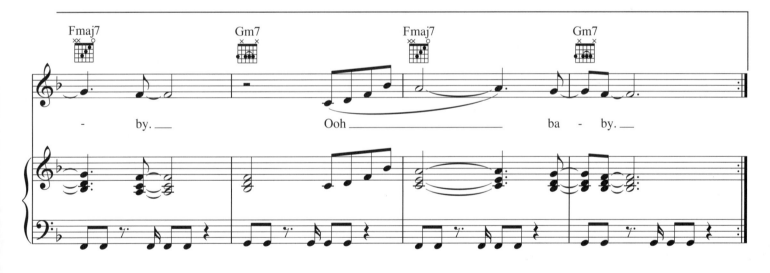

- by. ___ Ooh ___ ba - by. ___

come a - round? 'Cause I want to share for - ev - er with you, ba - by. ___

ANYTIME YOU NEED A FRIEND

Words and Music by MARIAH CAREY
and WALTER AFANASIEFF

If you're lone - ly and need a friend ___
When the shad - ows are clos - ing in ___

and trou - bles seem ___ like they nev - er end, ___
and your spir - it di - min - ish - ing, ___

just re - mem - ber to keep the faith ___
just re - mem - ber you're not a - lone ___

and love will be ___ there _____ to light the way. ___
and love will be ___ there _____ to guide you home. ___

An - y - time you need a friend, ___ I will be here. _____ You'll nev - er be a - lone a - gain, ___

___ so, don't you fear. _____ E - ven if you're miles a - way, ___

___ I'm by your side. _____ So, don't you ev - er be lone - ly.

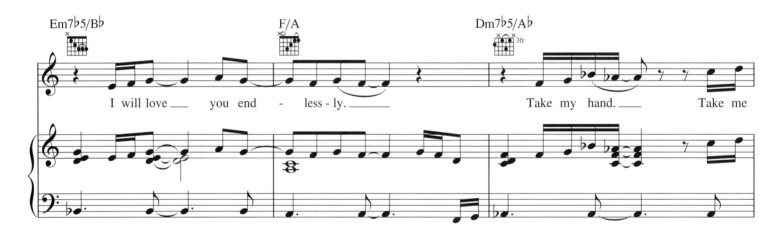

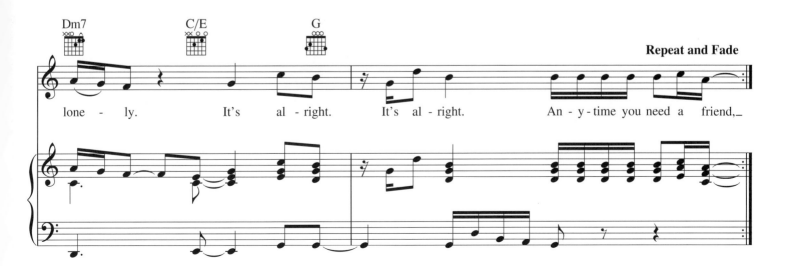

CAN'T LET GO

Lyrics by MARIAH CAREY
Music by MARIAH CAREY and WALTER AFANASIEFF

Moderately slow

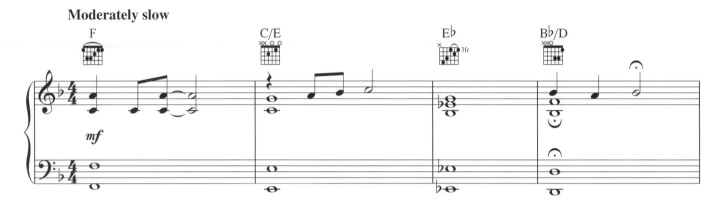

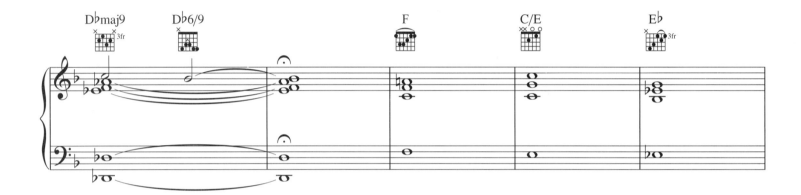

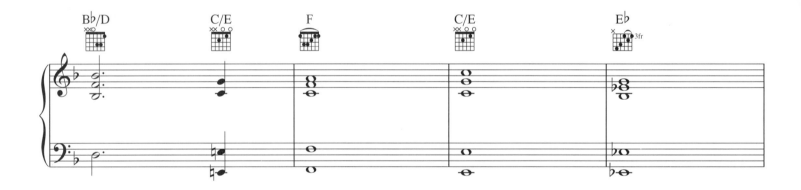

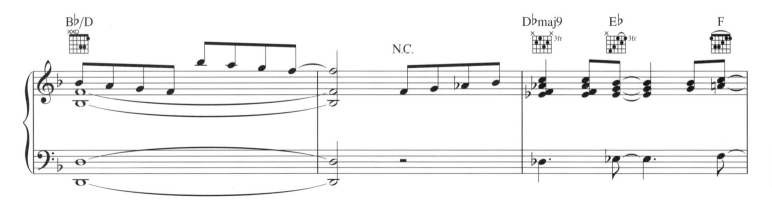

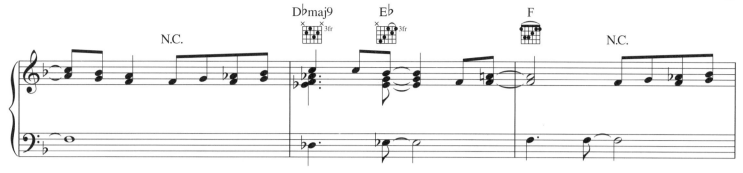

There you are _____
cast a - side, _____ you don't e - ven

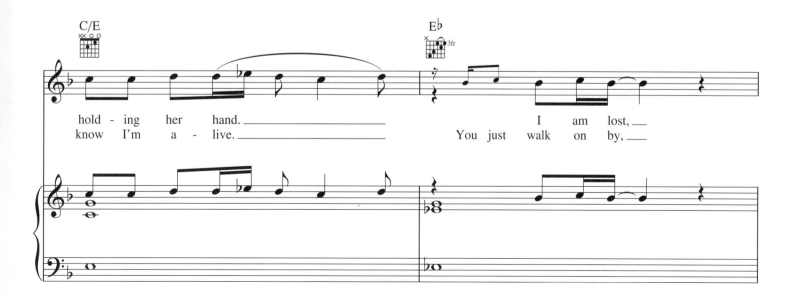

hold - ing her hand. _____   I am lost, ____
know I'm a - live. _____   You just walk on by, ____

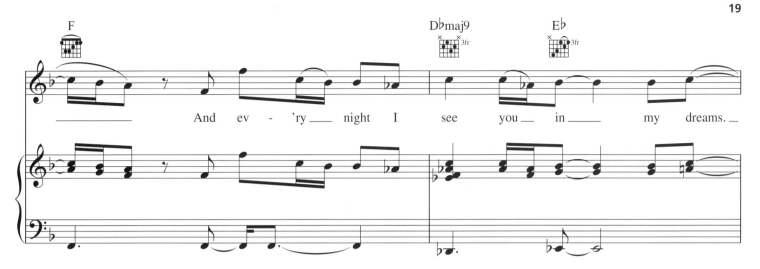

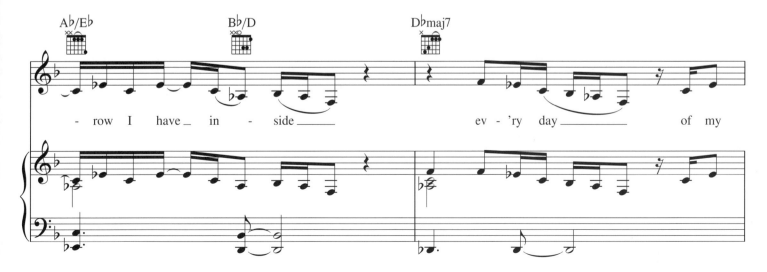

life?_____ Do you know the way it feels___ when all___

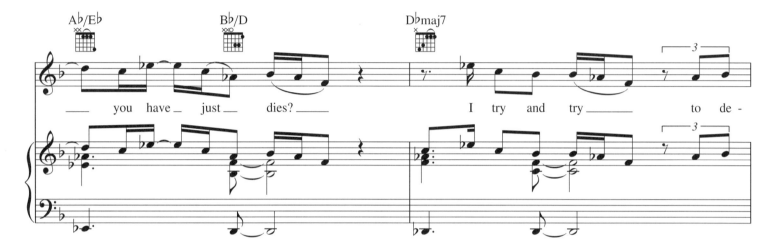

___ you have___ just___ dies?_____ I try and try_____ to de-

ny that I need you but still you re-main___ on my mind._____ E - ven though I

Oh, no I just can't get you out of my mind._____
try I can't___ let go._____

try I can't___ let go._____ Some - thing in your___

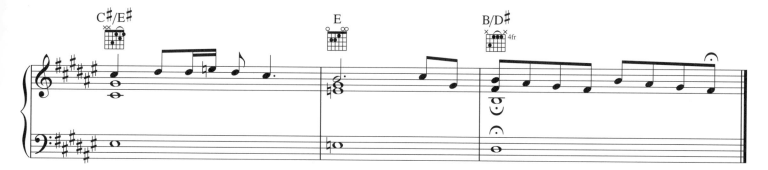

ENDLESS LOVE

Words and Music by
LIONEL RICHIE

Moderately slow

My love, ___ there's on-ly you in my life, ___
Two hearts, ___ two hearts that beat as ___ one; ___

the on-ly thing that's right. ___ My
our lives have just be-gun. ___ For-

first ___ love, ___ you're ev-'ry breath that I take, ___
ev-___ er, ___ I'll hold you close in my arms, ___

you're ev - 'ry step I make. ___
I can't re - sist your charms. ___
And
And

I,
love,

I ___ want to share all my
I'll be a fool for

love ___ with you;
you, ___ I'm ___ sure;

no one else ___
you ___ know I don't

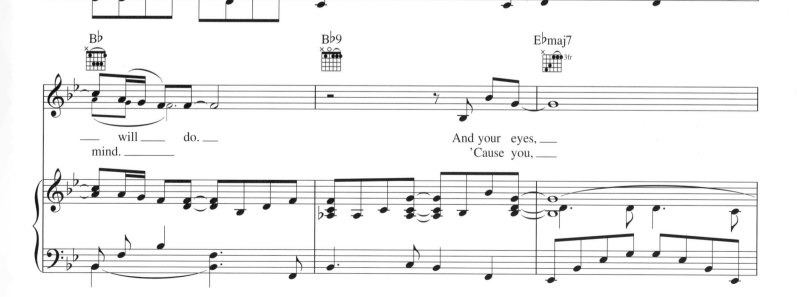

___ will ___ do. ___
mind. ___

And your eyes, ___
'Cause you, ___

they tell me how much you care.
you mean the world to me. Oh,

yes, you will al - ways be
I know I've found in you

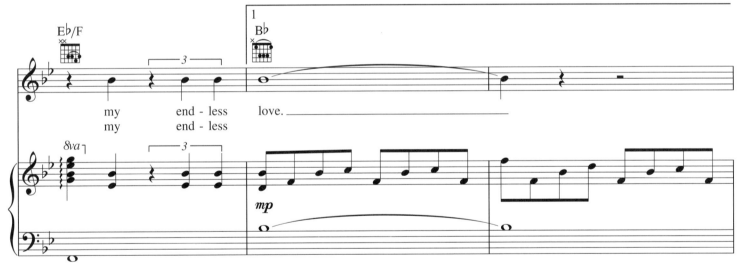

my end - less love.
my end - less

love.

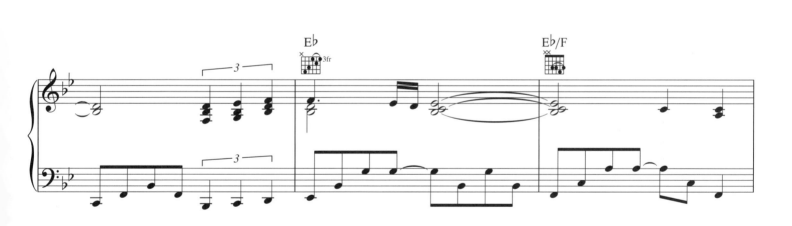

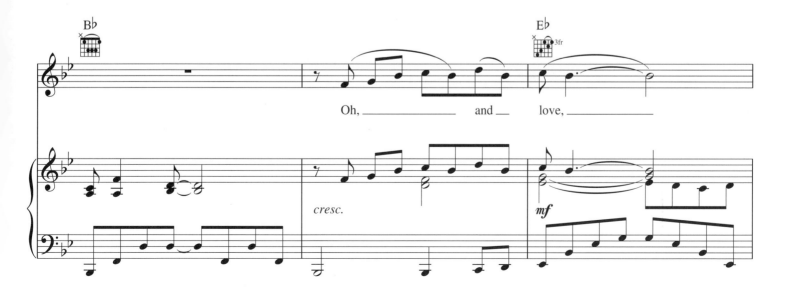

Oh, _____ and _____ love, _____

cresc.

mf

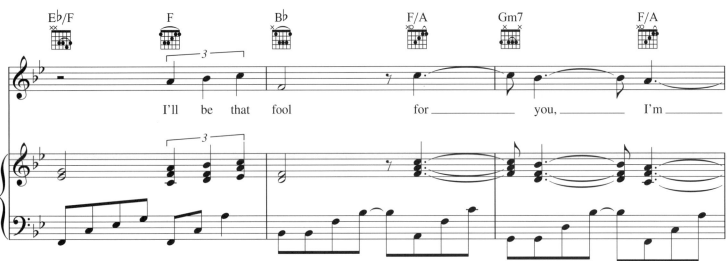

I'll be that fool for _____ you, _____ I'm

_____ sure; _____ you __ know I don't mind. _____

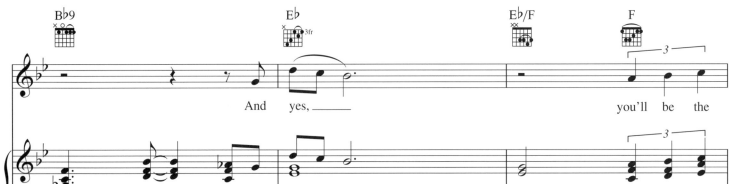

And yes, _____ you'll be the

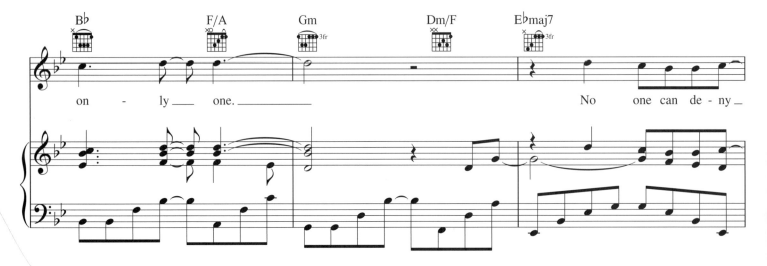

on - ly __ one. _____ No one can de - ny __

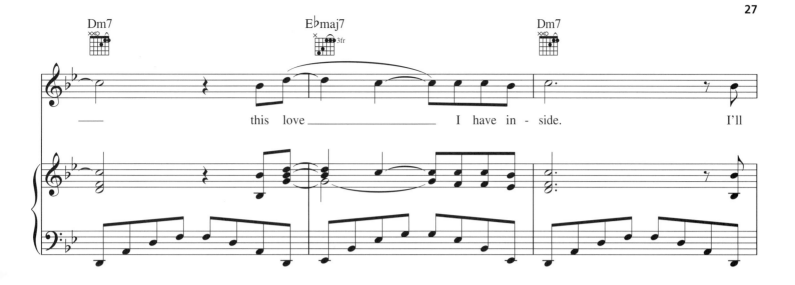

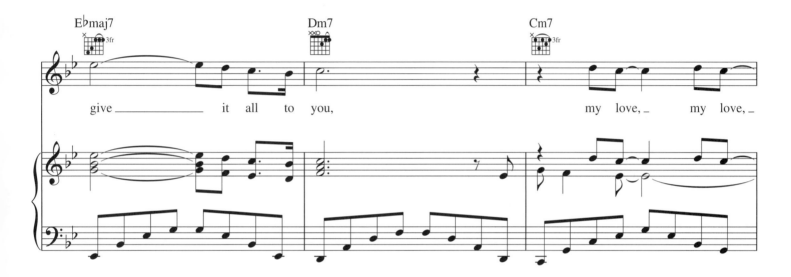

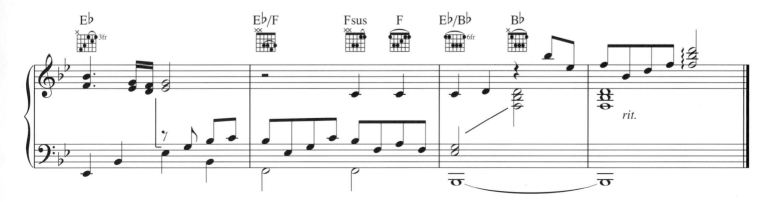

HERO

Words and Music by MARIAH CAREY
and WALTER AFANASIEFF

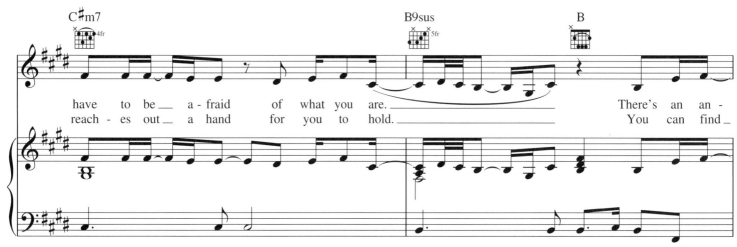

and you'll fi - n'ly see __ the truth __ that a he - ro lies __ in you. __

It's a __

Lord knows _____ dreams are hard __ to fol - low,

but don't let an - y - one __ tear them a - way. __ Hold __ on, _____

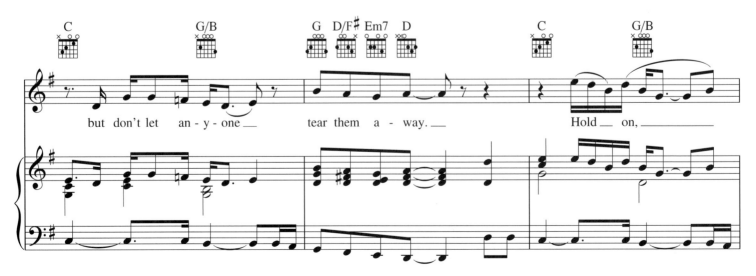

D.S. al Coda

there will be __ to - mor - row. In __ time __ you'll find the way.

rall.

CODA

That a he - ro lies in

molto rall.

you, ___

a tempo

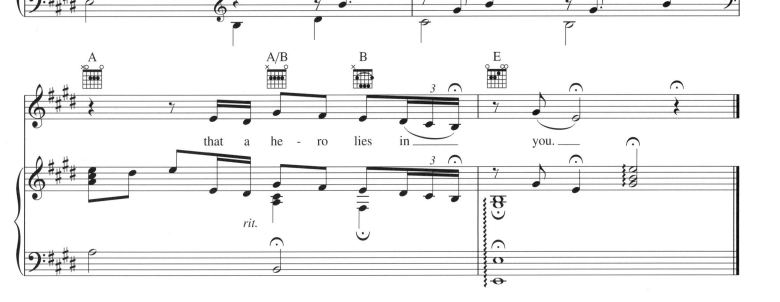

that a he - ro lies in __ you. __

rit.

HOW MUCH
(How Much I Love You)

Words and Music by MARIAH CAREY,
JERMAINE DUPRI, BRYAN MICHAEL COX, TUPAC SHAKUR,
TYRONE WRICE, RICKY ROUSE and DARRYL HARPER

Moderately fast

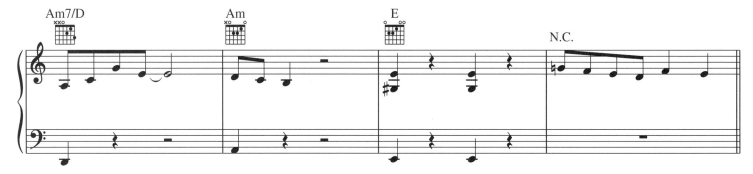

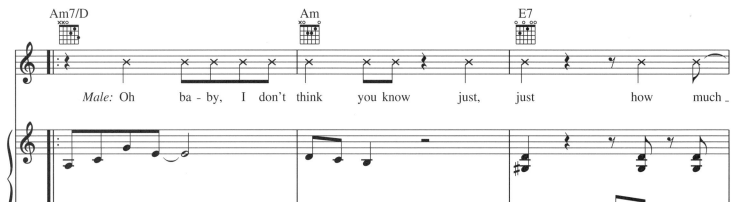

Male: Oh ba-by, I don't think you know just, just how much ___ I love ___ you. Have you ev-er felt lone-ly when you know you got-ta leave me?

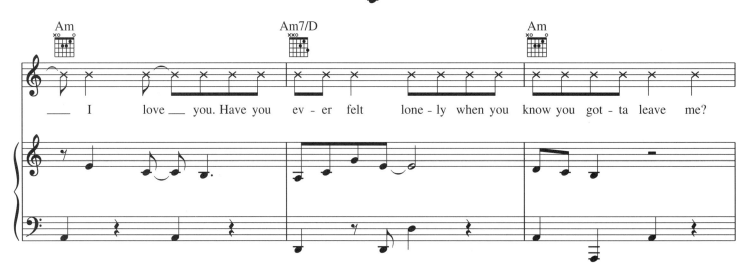

Original key: A-flat minor. This edition has been transposed up one half-step to be more playable.

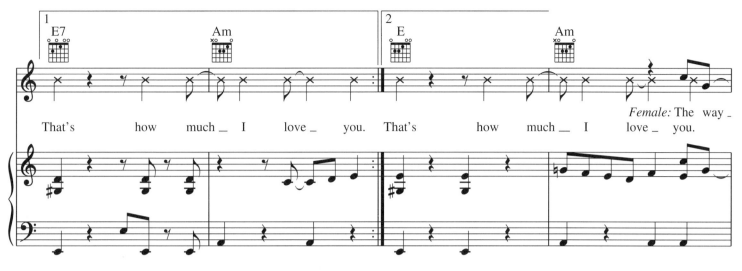

That's how much __ I love __ you. That's how much __ I love __ you.

Female: The way __

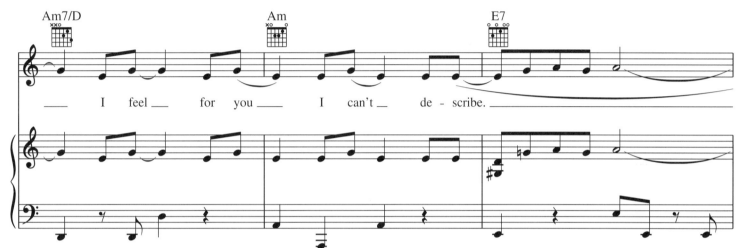

__ I feel __ for you __ I can't __ de - scribe. _____

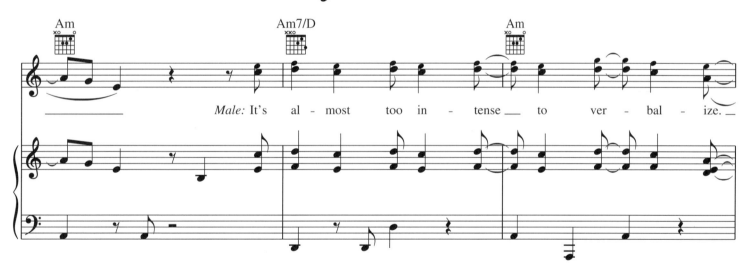

_____ *Male:* It's al - most too in - tense __ to ver - bal - ize. __

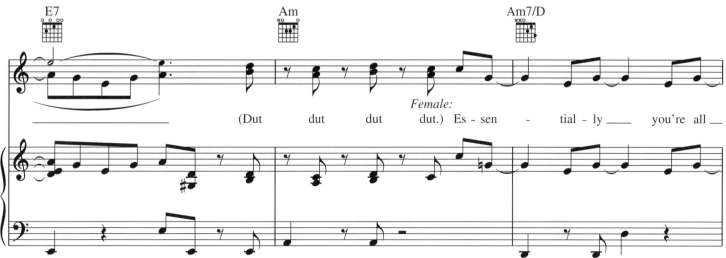

_____ (Dut dut dut dut.) *Female:* Es - sen - tial - ly ____ you're all __

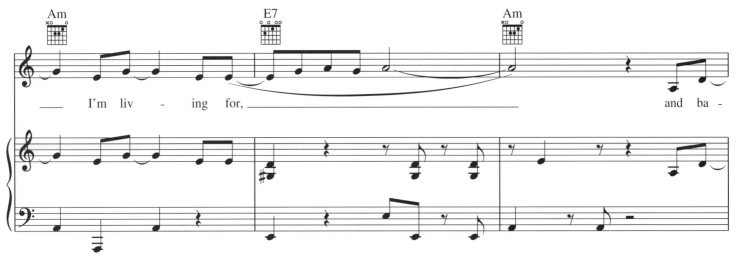

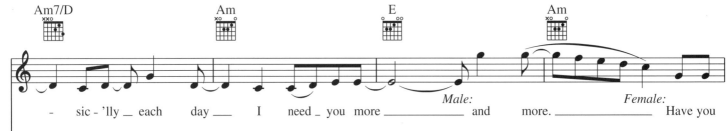

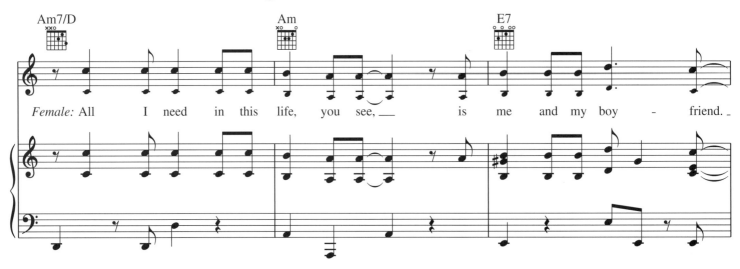

it's ob - vi - ous _ these feel - ings _ run _ so deep. _____

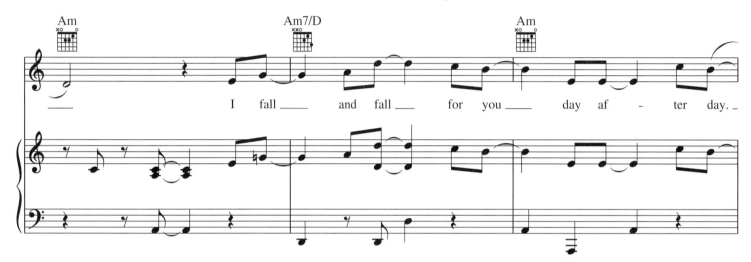

____ I fall ____ and fall ____ for you ____ day af - ter day. _

Male:
_____ (Dut dut dut dut.) No - bod - y else __ could ev -

Female:

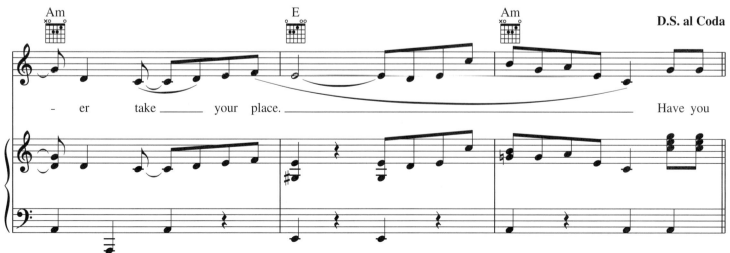

D.S. al Coda

- er take _____ your place. _____ Have you

CODA

You don't got-ta waste your time ___ and wor - ry;

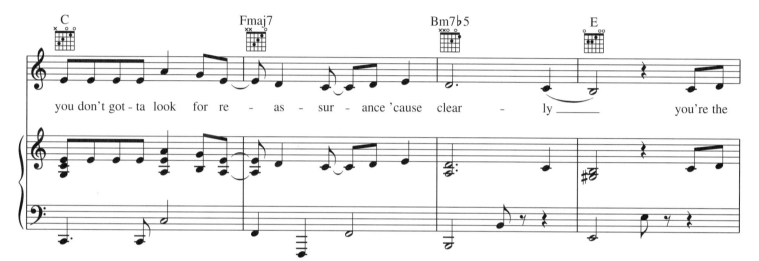

you don't got-ta look for re - as - sur - ance 'cause clear - ly ___ you're the

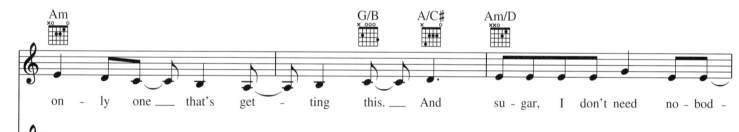

on - ly one ___ that's get - ting this. ___ And su - gar, I don't need no - bod -

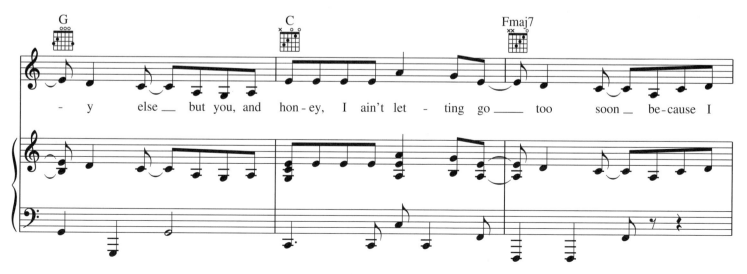

- y else ___ but you, and hon - ey, I ain't let - ting go ___ too soon ___ be-cause I

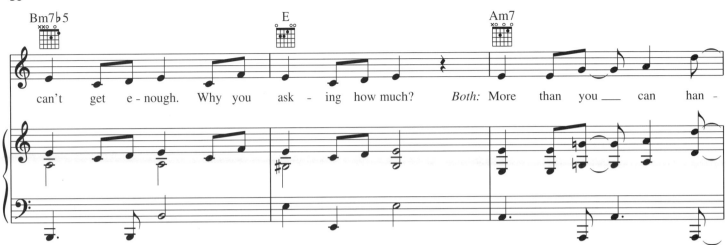

can't get e - nough. Why you ask - ing how much? *Both:* More than you ___ can han -

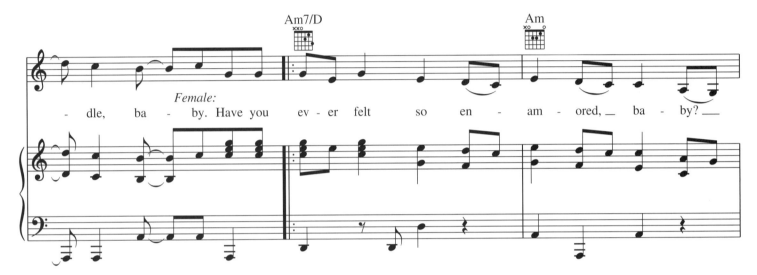

Female:
- dle, ba - by. Have you ev - er felt so en - am - ored, ___ ba - by? ___

Male:
That's how much ___ I love ___ you. *Female:* All I need in this

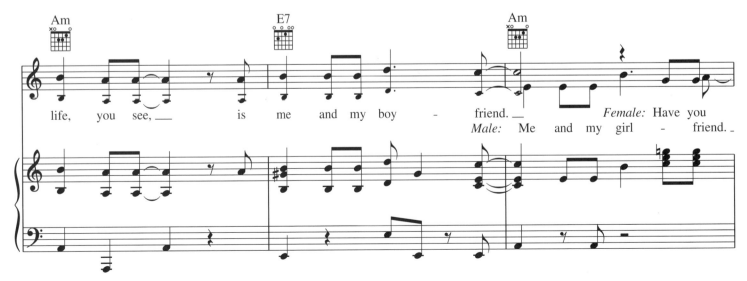

life, you see, ___ is me and my boy - friend. ___ *Female:* Have you
Male: Me and my girl - friend. ___

I STILL BELIEVE

Words and Music by BEPPE CANTARELLI
and ANTONINA ARMATO

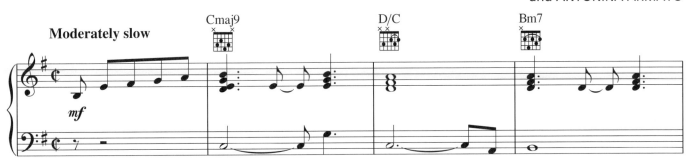

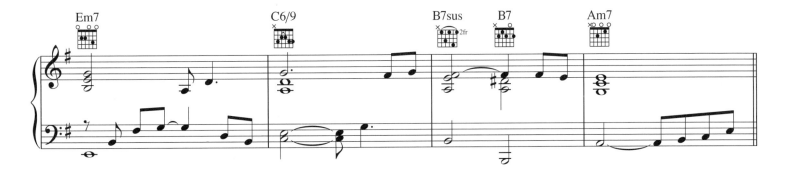

You look in my eyes _____ and I get e-mo-tion-al ____
I'm filled with all ____ the joy ____

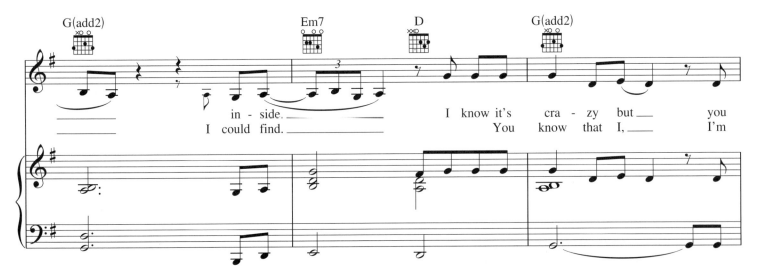

in-side. _____
I could find. _____
I know it's cra-zy but ____ you
You know that I, ____ I'm

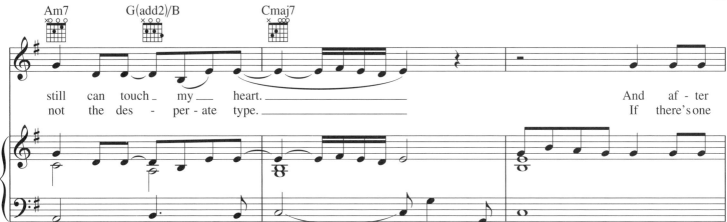

still can touch __ my __ heart. _____ And af - ter
not the des - per - ate type. _____ If there's one

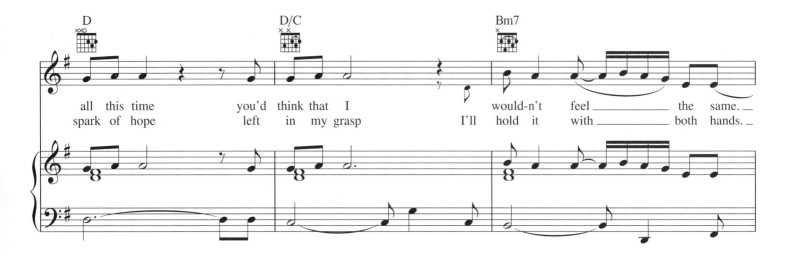

all this time _____ you'd think that I _____ would-n't feel _____ the same. __
spark of hope _____ left in my grasp _____ I'll hold it with _____ both hands. __

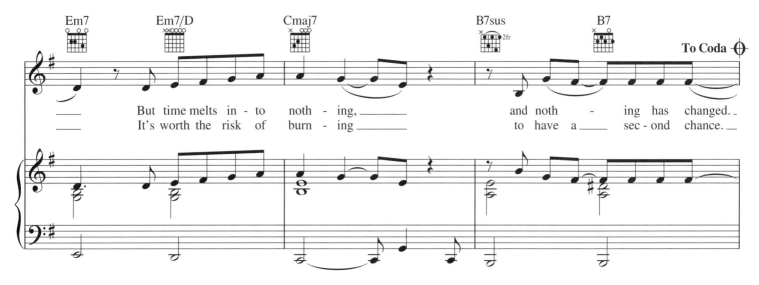

To Coda ⊕

But time melts in - to noth - ing, _____ and noth - ing has changed. __
It's worth the risk of burn - ing _____ to have a __ sec - ond chance. __

I still be - lieve _____

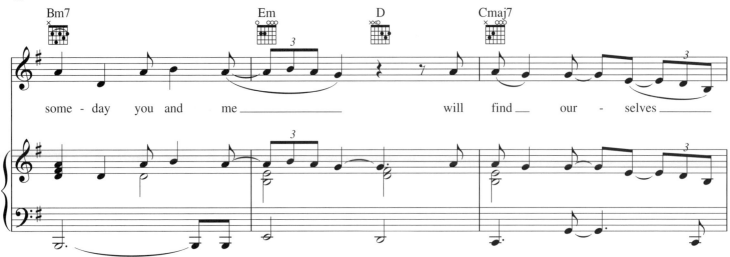

some-day you and me _____ will find _ our - selves _____

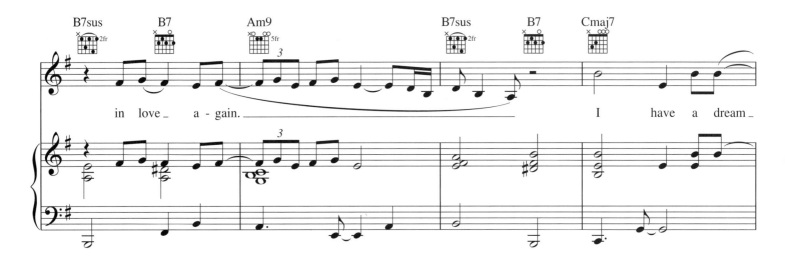

in love _ a - gain. _____ I have a dream _

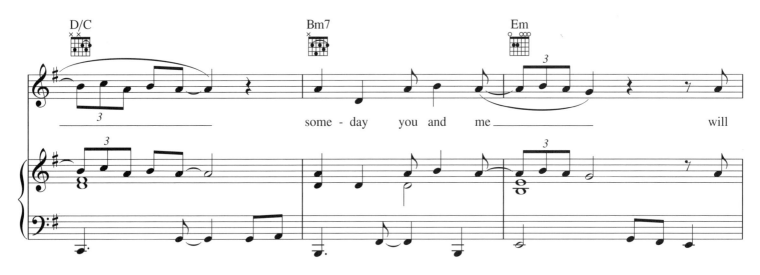

_____ some - day you and me _____ will

find _ our - selves _____ in love _ a - gain.

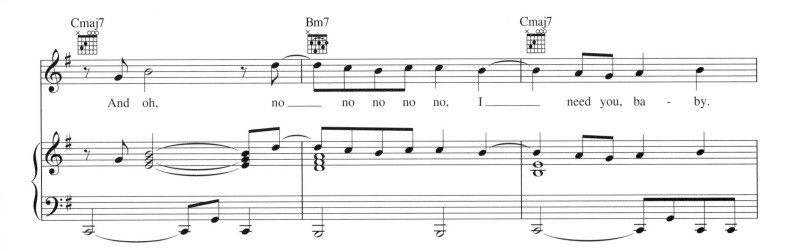

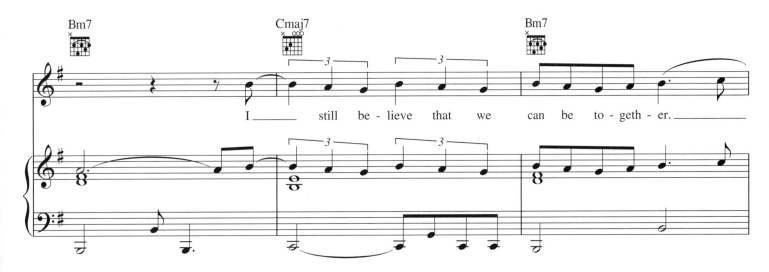

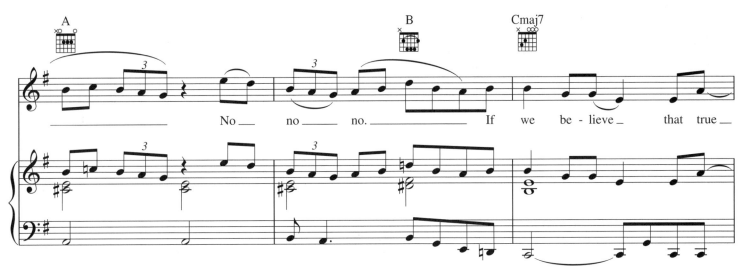

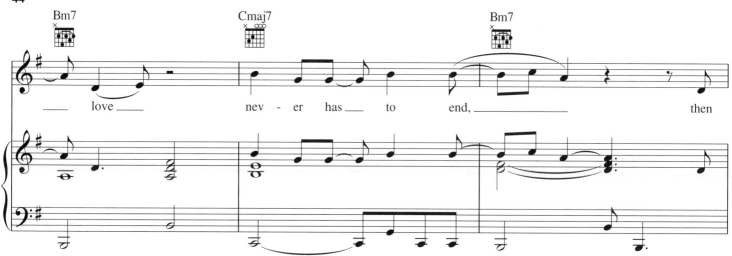

love _____ nev - er has _____ to end, _____ then

we must know that we _____ will love _____ a - gain. _____

Oh, _____ I still be - lieve _____

some - day you and me _____ will find _____ our - selves _____

in love __ a - gain. _____ Oh, ba - by, yeah __ yeah.

I __ had a dream _____ you _____ and

me _____ will find our - selves __ in love __ a - gain. __

Repeat and Fade

Optional Ending

I'LL BE THERE

Words and Music by BERRY GORDY,
HAL DAVIS, WILLIE HUTCH and BOB WEST

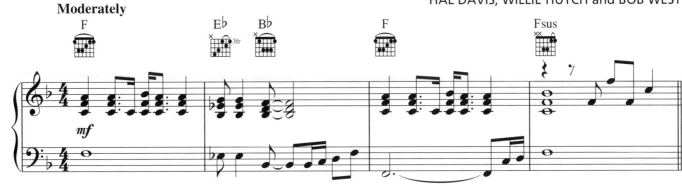

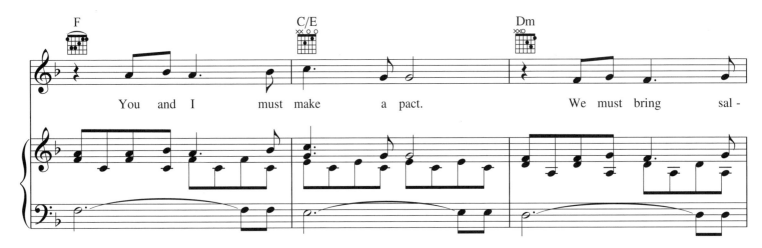

You and I must make a pact. We must bring sal-

va - tion back. _____ Where there is love, _____ I'll _____

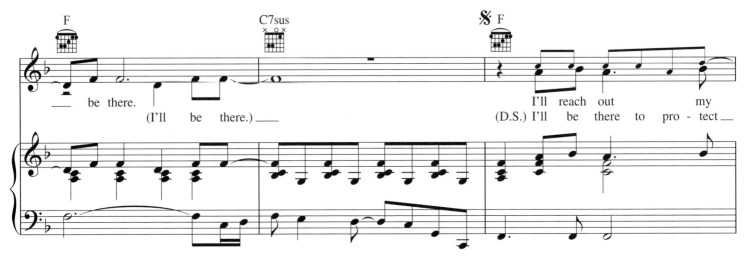

___ be there. I'll be there. _____ I'll reach out my

(I'll be there.) _____ (D.S.) I'll be there to pro - tect ___

you know I'll keep hold-ing on. ___ Let me fill your heart ___ with joy and laugh-ter.

To-geth-er-ness, well, it's all I'm af - ter. ___ Just call my

name ___ and I'll ___ be there.

(I'll be there.) ___

D.S. al Coda

hold - ing on. ___

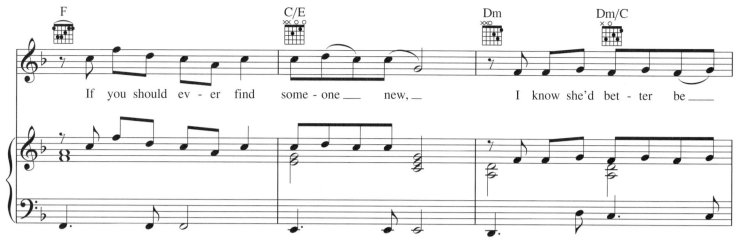

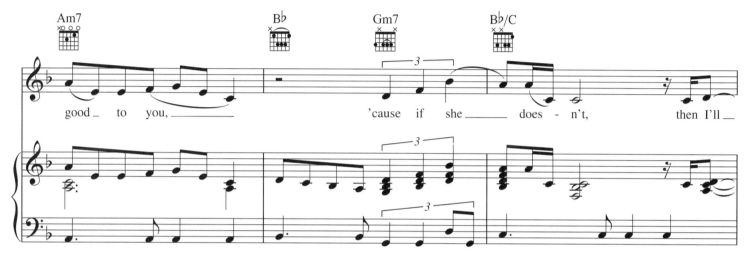

Just call my name _____ and I'll ___ be there. ___

Just call my name _____

and I'll ___ be there. _____

a tempo

molto rit.

LOVE TAKES TIME

Words and Music by MARIAH CAREY
and BEN MARGULIES

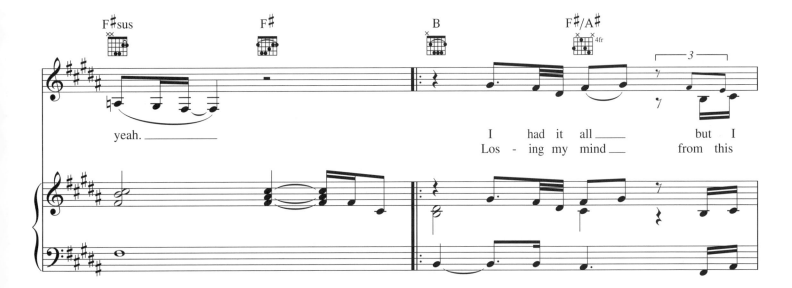

wrong.
- com - plete, _____ yeah. _____
Lord, I'm need - ing you now. _____

Now I wan-der a - round _____ feel-ing
Tell me

down _____ and cold, _____

how _____ to stop the _____ rain.

try - ing to be - lieve _____ that _____

Tears are fall-ing down _____ end - less -

_____ you're gone.
ly.

Whoa. _____

Love takes time to heal _____

when you're hurt-ing so ___ much. Could-n't see that I _____ was blind ___ to

let you ___ go.___ I can't es-cape the pain _____ in - side _____ 'cause

love ___ takes ___ time.___ I don't want to be here.

I don't want to be ___ here ___ a - lone. ___ Ooh. ___

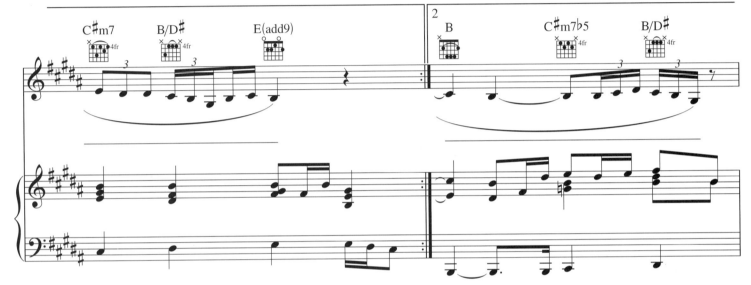

You might say ___ that it's o - ver. ___

You might say ___ that you don't ___ care. ___ Oh. ___

MY ALL

Words and Music by MARIAH CAREY
and WALTER AFANASIEFF

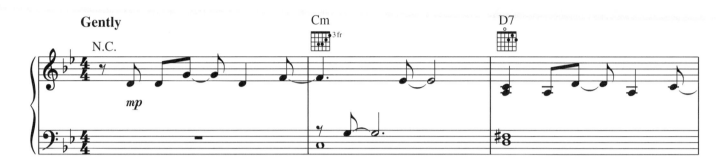

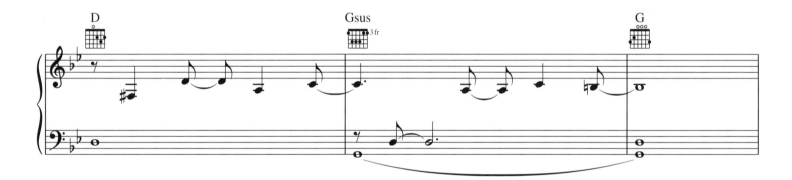

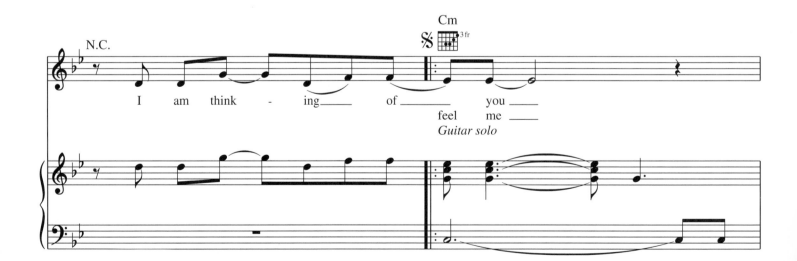

I am think-ing____ of ____ you ____

feel me ____

Guitar solo

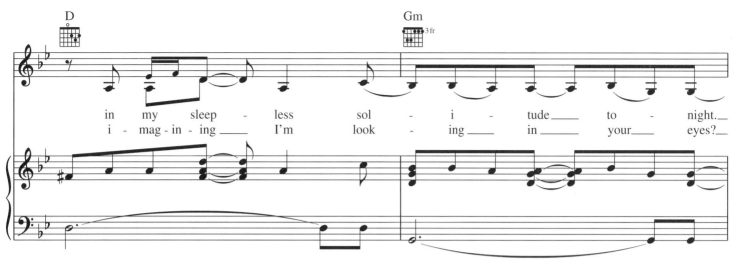

in my sleep - less sol - i - tude to - night.
i - mag - in - ing I'm look - ing in your eyes?

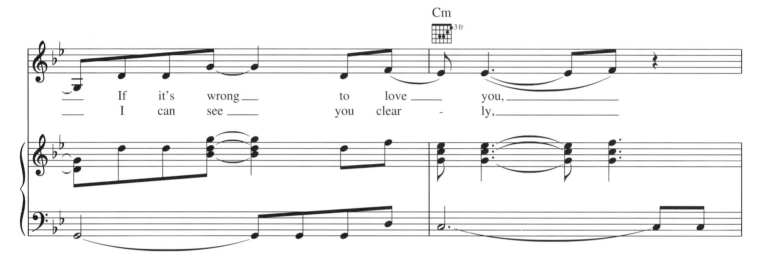

If it's wrong to love you,
I can see you clear - ly,

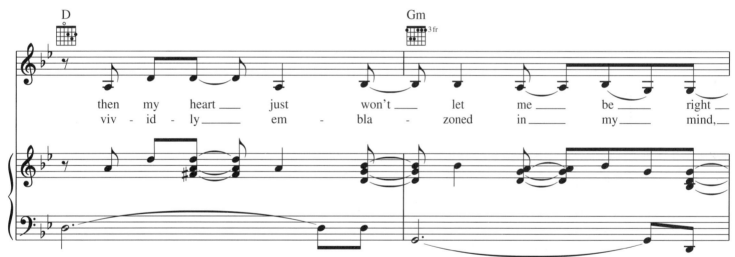

then my heart just won't let me be right
viv - id - ly em - bla - zoned in my mind,

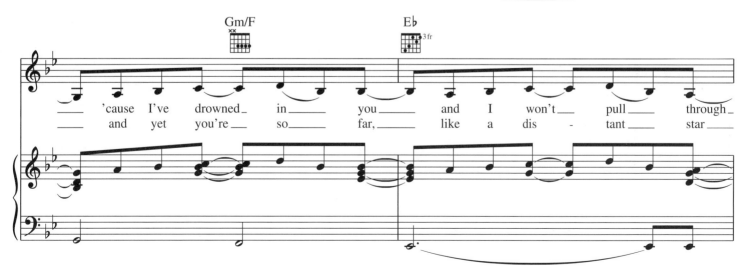

'cause I've drowned in you and I won't pull through
and yet you're so far, like a dis - tant star

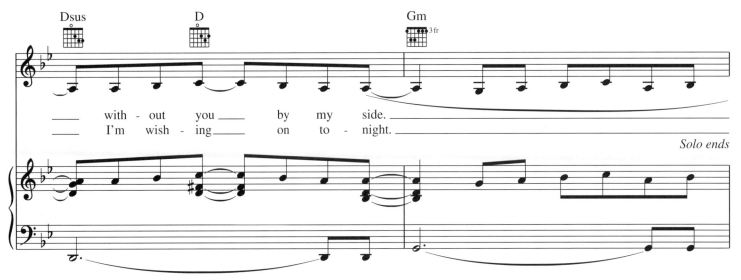

with - out you ___ by my side. ___
I'm wish - ing ___ on to - night. ___

Solo ends

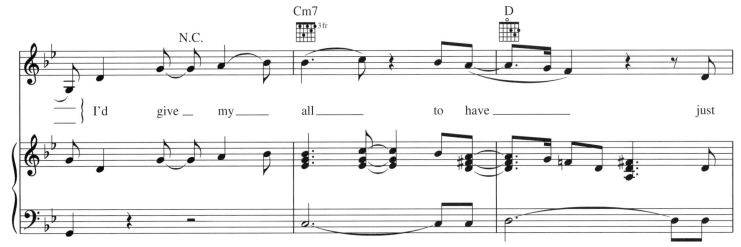

I'd give ___ my ___ all ___ to have ___ just

one more night ___ with ___ you. I'd risk ___ my ___ life ___ to feel ___

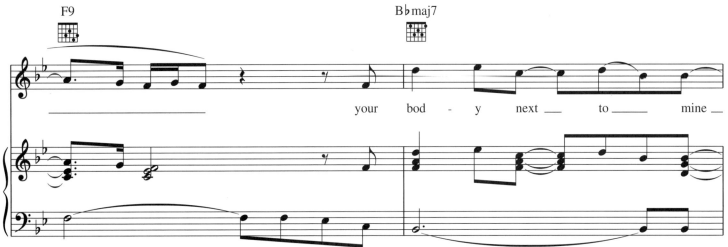

___ your bod - y next ___ to ___ mine ___

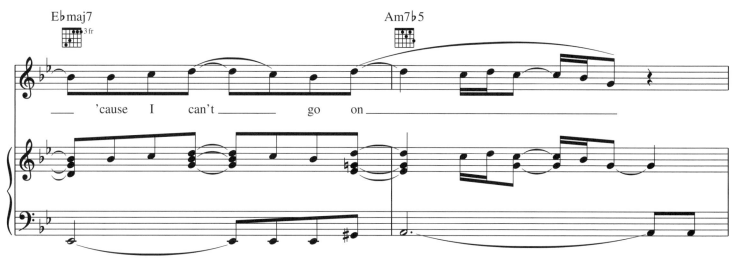

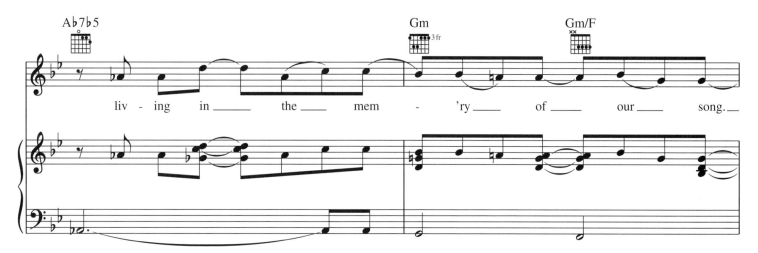

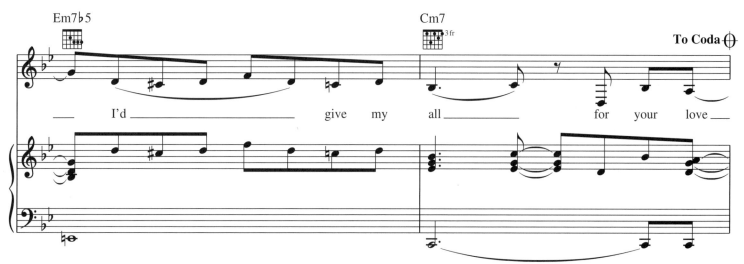

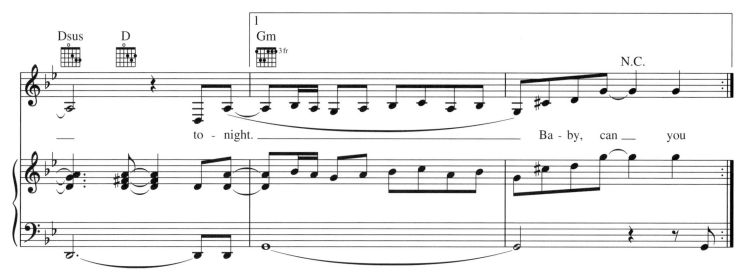

D.S. al Coda

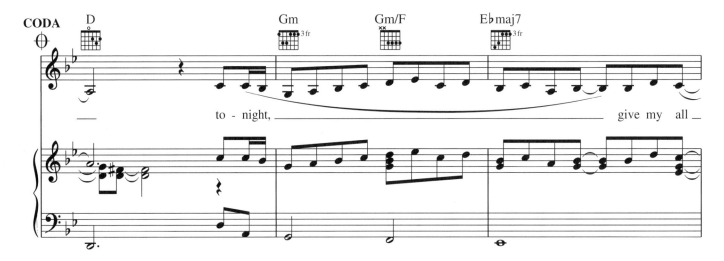

to - night, _____ give my all ___

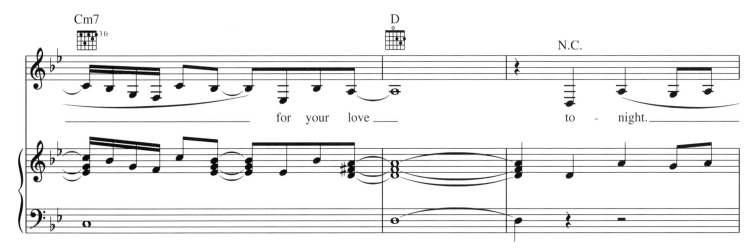

_____ for your love ___ to - night. ___

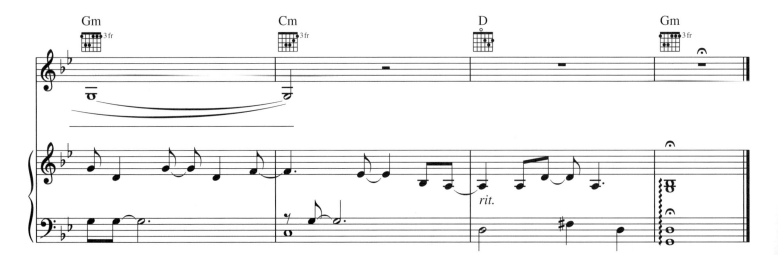

ONE SWEET DAY

Words and Music by MARIAH CAREY, WALTER AFANASIEFF,
MICHAEL McCARY, NATHAN MORRIS, SHAWN STOCKMAN,
and WANYA MORRIS

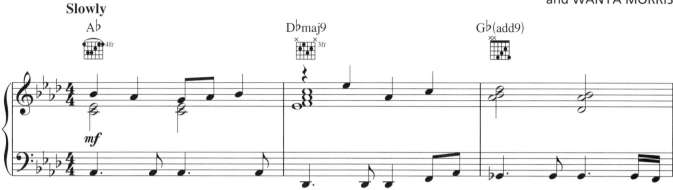

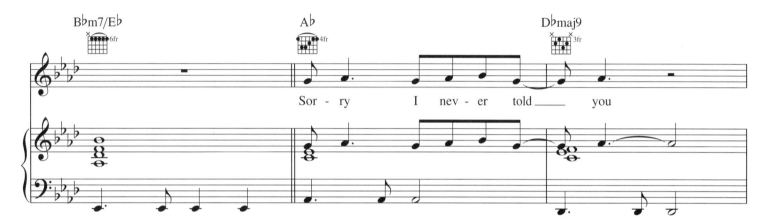

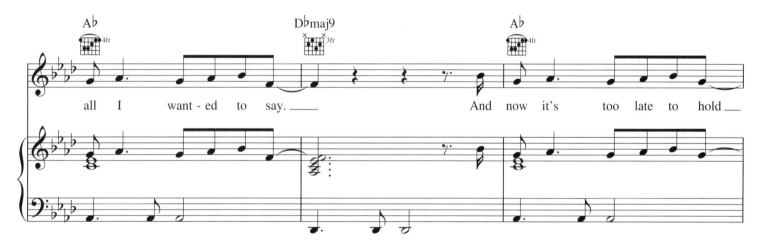

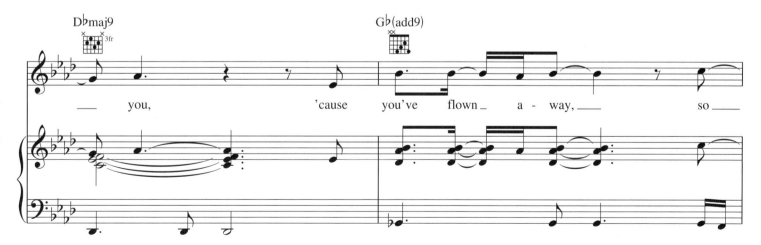

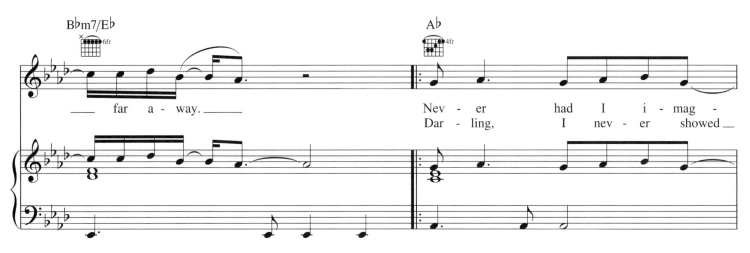

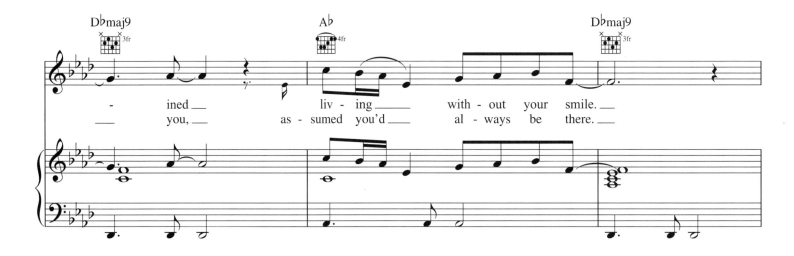

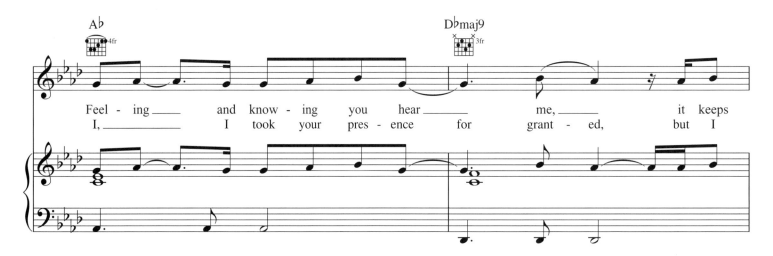

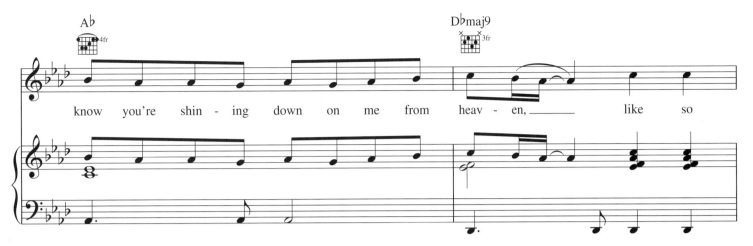

know you're shin - ing down on me from heav - en, _____ like so

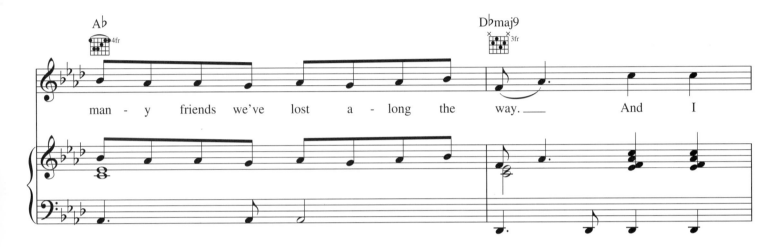

man - y friends we've lost a - long the way. _____ And I

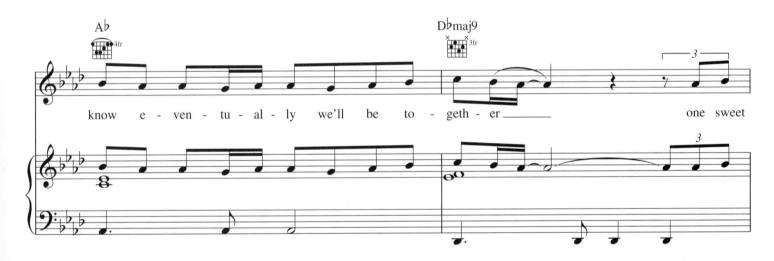

know e - ven - tu - al - ly we'll be to - geth - er _____ one sweet

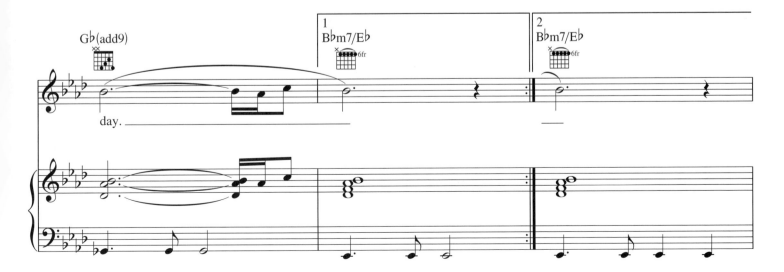

day. _____

Although the sun will nev - er shine _ the same, _

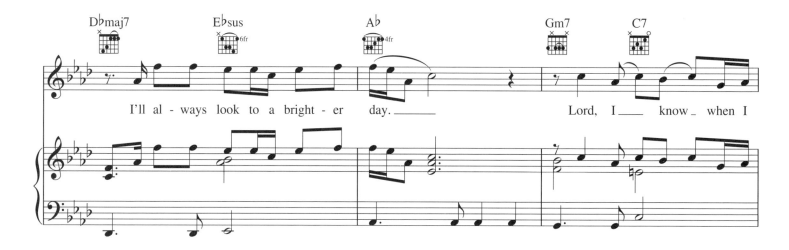

I'll al - ways look to a bright - er day. _____ Lord, I ____ know _ when I

lay me down to sleep, _____ you will al - ways lis - ten _____ as I

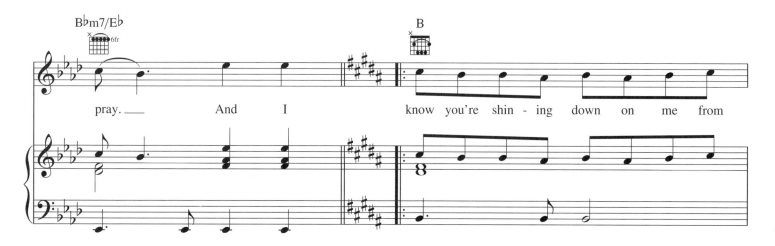

pray. ___ And I know you're shin - ing down on me from

heav - en, _____ like so man - y friends we've lost a - long the way. _ And I

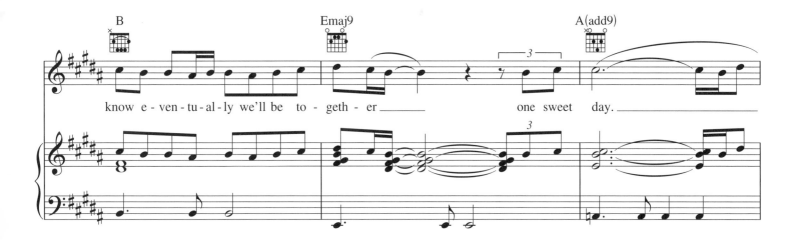

know e - ven - tu - al - ly we'll be to - geth - er _____ one sweet day. _____

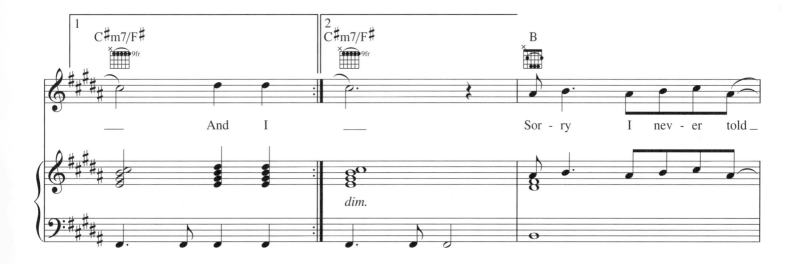

_ And I _ Sor - ry I nev - er told _

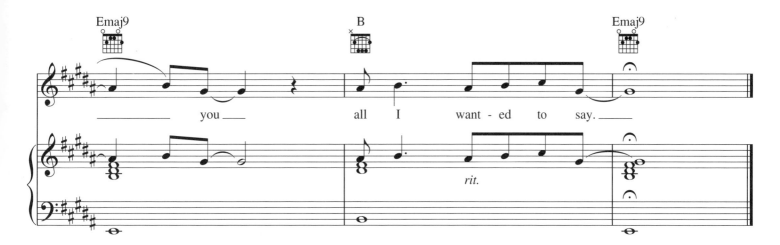

_____ you _ all I want - ed to say. _____

REFLECTIONS
(Care Enough)
from GLITTER

Words and Music by MARIAH CAREY
and PHILIPPE PIERRE

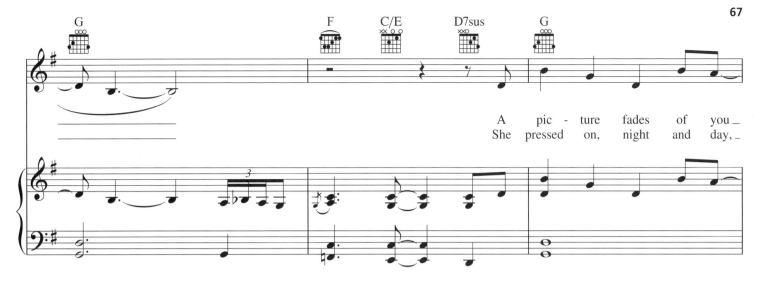

A pic-ture fades of you __
She pressed on, night and day, __

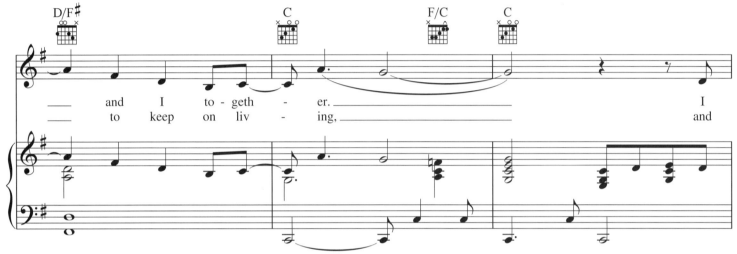

__ and I to-geth - er. _____
__ to keep on liv - ing, _____ I and

have - n't come __ to terms __ with how __ we said __ good - bye. __
tried so man - y ways __ to keep __ her soul __ a - live. __

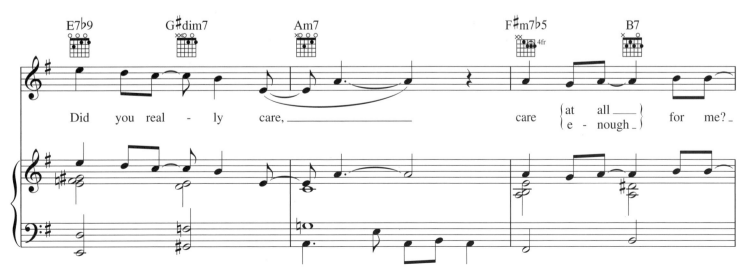

Did you real - ly care, _____ care {at all __ } {e - nough _ } for me? _

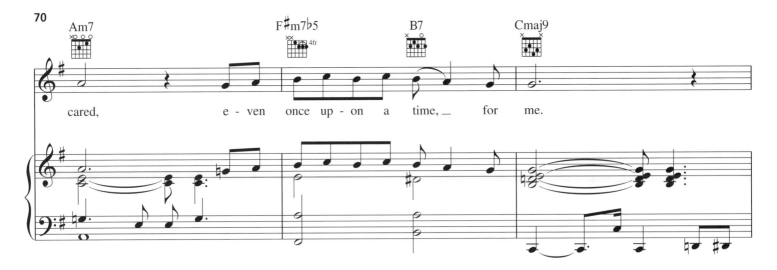

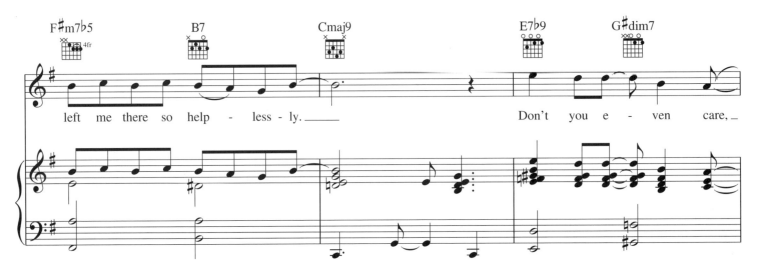

THE ROOF

Words and Music by MARIAH CAREY,
ALBERT JOHNSON, KEJUAN MUCHITA, MARK ROONEY,
SAMUEL BARNES and JEAN OLIVIER

Moderately, not too fast

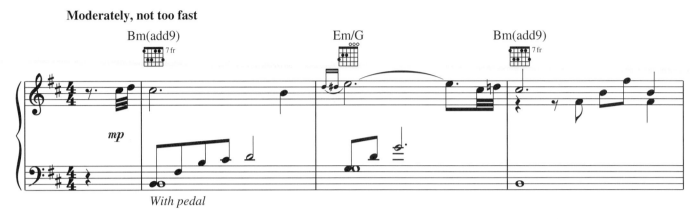

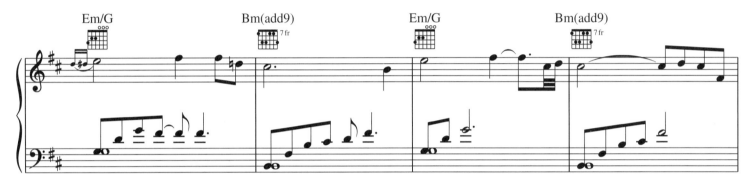

Same tempo, R & B Shuffle

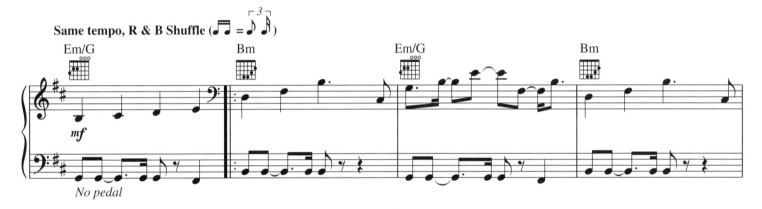

It was-n't rain-ing yet, _____ but it was def-i-nite-

-ly a lit -tle mist - y on __ that warm __ No - vem - ber night. __

_____ And my heart was pound - ing, ___ my in - ner voice re-sound -

- ing, ___ beg-ging me __ to turn __ a - way, __ but I ___ just had __

___ to see __ your face __ to feel __ a - live. _____ And then __ you cas -

- u - 'lly ___ walked in ___ the room, _____ and I ___ was twist -
- ly pressed ___ your lips ___ to mine, _____ and feel - ings sur -

- ed in ___ the web ___ of my ___ de - sire for you. My ap - pre - hen -
- faced I'd sup - pressed ___ for such ___ a long, long time. And for ___ a - while, ___

- sion blew ___ a - way. ___ I on - ly want - ed you ___ to taste ___ my sad -
_____ I ___ for - got ___ the sor - row and the pain ___ and melt - ed with ___

- ness as ___ you kissed ___ me in ___ the dark. Ev - 'ry time   I
___ you as ___ we stood ___ there in ___ the rain. _____

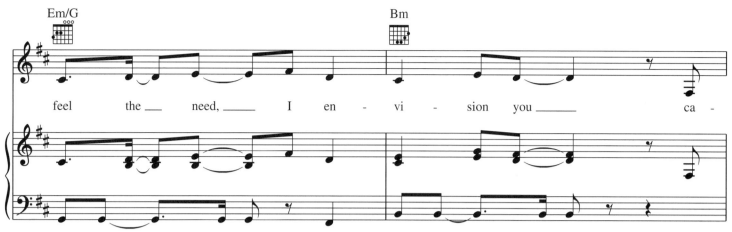

feel the ___ need, ___ I en - vi - sion you ___ ca -

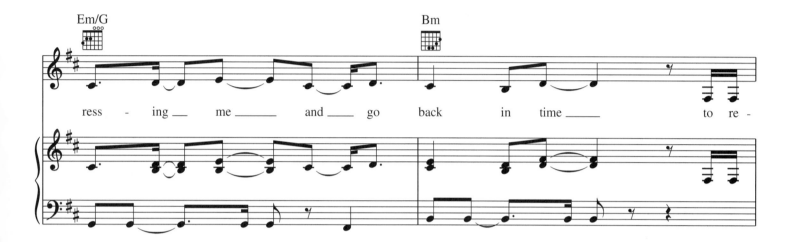

ress - ing ___ me ___ and ___ go back in time ___ to re -

To Coda

live the ___ splen - dor of you ___ and I ___ on the

And so ___ we fin - ished the ___ Mo - et and

roof - top ___ that ___ rain - y night. ___ I start - ed

feel - ing lib - er - a - ted, and I sur - ren - dered as __ you took __ me in __ your arms. __

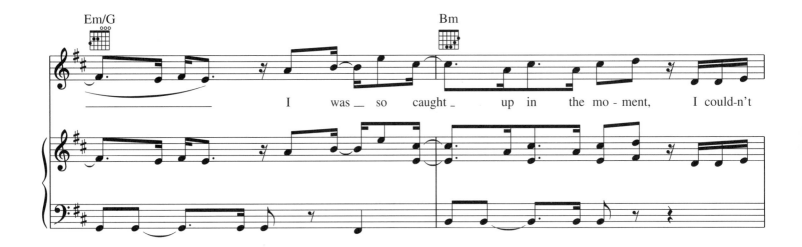

_____ I was __ so caught __ up in the mo - ment, I could-n't

bear to let __ you go __ yet, so I threw cau - tion to __ the wind __ and start - ed lis -

D.S. al Coda

- ten - ing __ to my long - ing heart. _____ And then __ you soft -

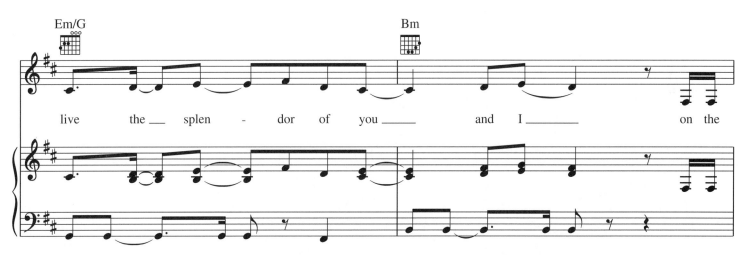

whis - pered the words "I love you" and touched you

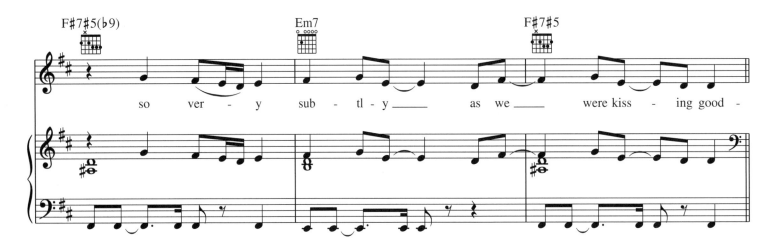

so ver - y sub - tl - y _____ as we _____ were kiss - ing good -

(1st x only) bye. _____

(Pret-ty ba - by, _____ how I'm miss - ing you.) _____

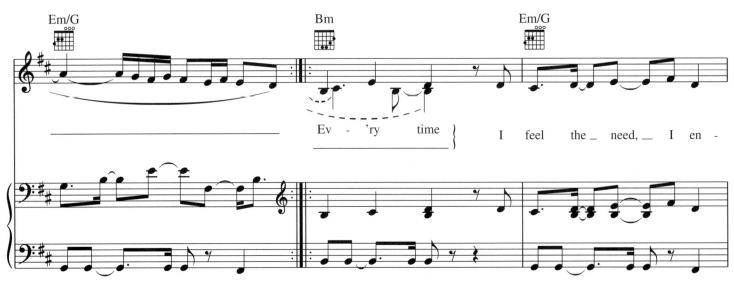

_____ Ev - 'ry time I feel the _ need, _ I en -

vi - sion you ___ ca - ress - ing _ me ___ and _ go back in time ___ to re -

live the ___ splen - dor of you ___ and I ___ on the

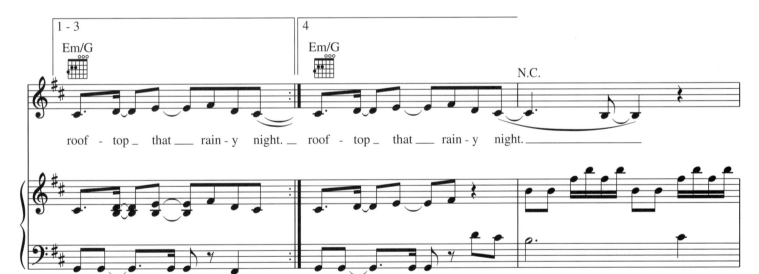

roof - top _ that ___ rain - y night. ___ roof - top _ that ___ rain - y night. ___

THANK GOD I FOUND YOU

Words and Music by MARIAH CAREY,
JAMES HARRIS III and TERRY LEWIS

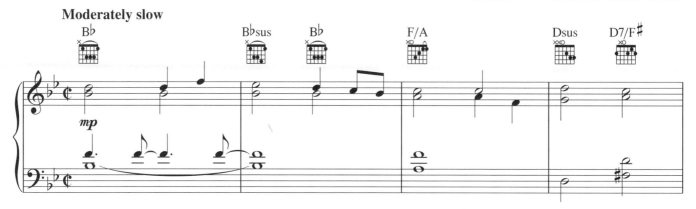

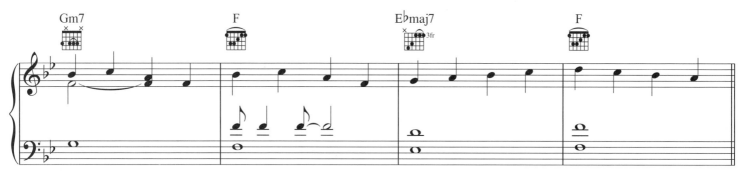

Female: I would give up ev-'ry-thing __ be-fore I'd sep-a-rate __
Male: And I will give you ev-'ry-thing; __ there's noth-ing in this world __

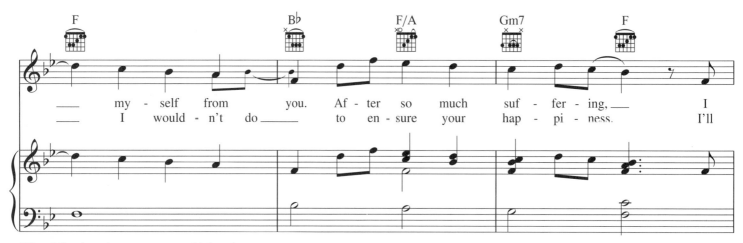

__ my-self from you. Af-ter so much suf-fer-ing, __ I
__ I would-n't do __ to en-sure your hap-pi-ness. I'll

*Vocal line is written one octave higher than sung.

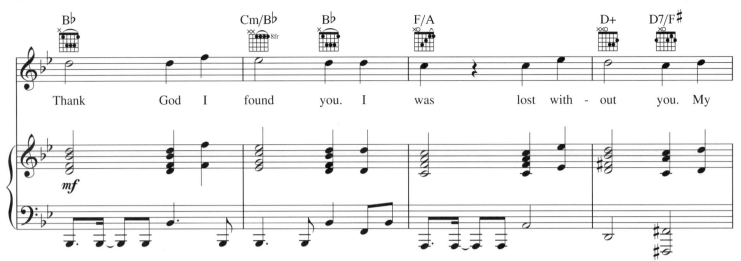

Thank God I found you. I was lost with - out you. My

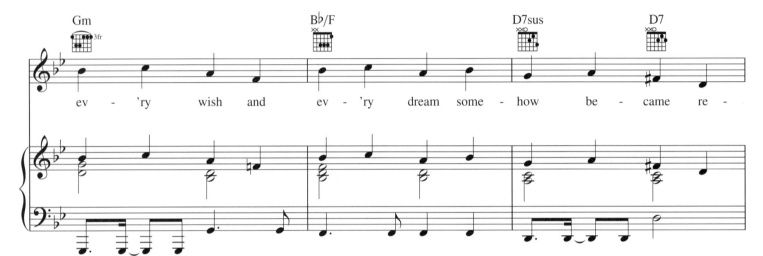

ev - 'ry wish and ev - 'ry dream some - how be - came re -

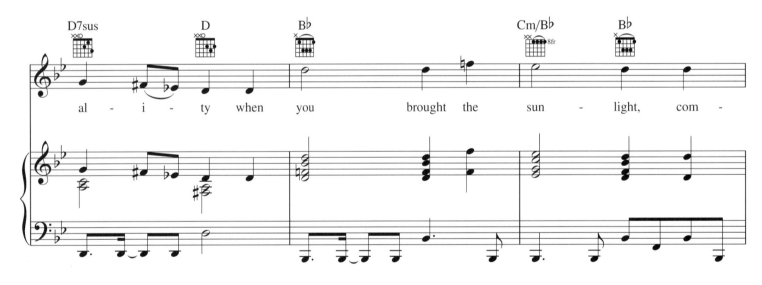

al - i - ty when you brought the sun - light, com -

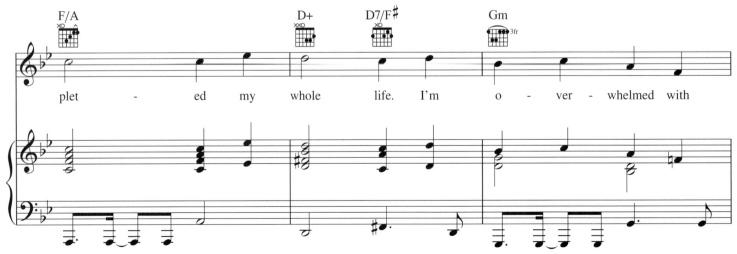

plet - ed my whole life. I'm o - ver - whelmed with

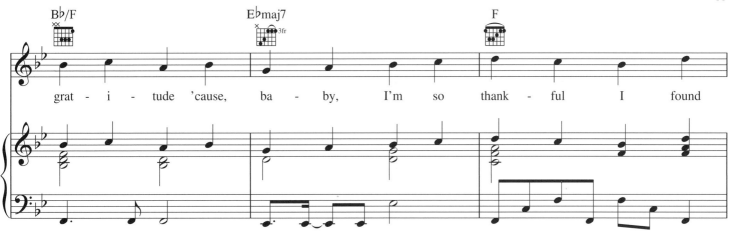

grat - i - tude 'cause, ba - by, I'm so thank - ful I found

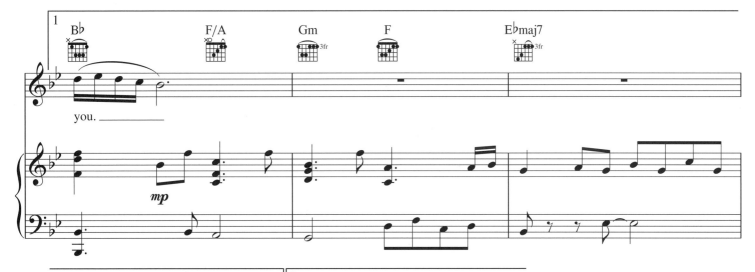

you. _____

you. _____ See... _____

Female: See, I

was _____ so des - o - late _____ be - fore _____ you came _____

to me. Look-ing back, *Male:* I guess it shows

Bkgd: Look-ing back...

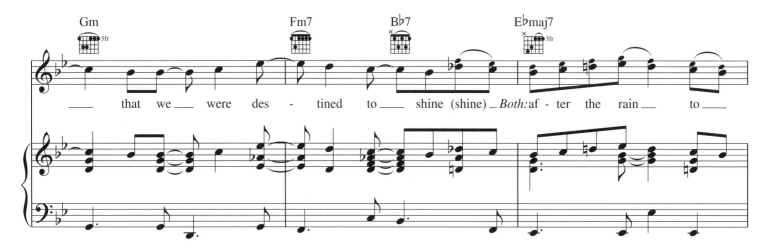

that we were des-tined to shine (shine) *Both:* af-ter the rain to

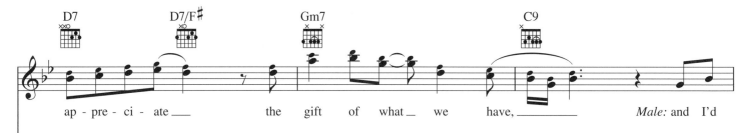

ap-pre-ci-ate the gift of what we have, *Male:* and I'd

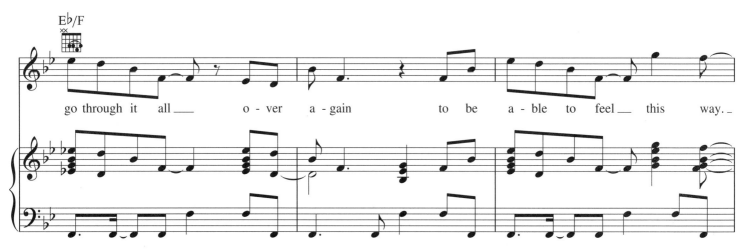

go through it all o-ver a-gain to be a-ble to feel this way.

Thank ___ God I found you. I

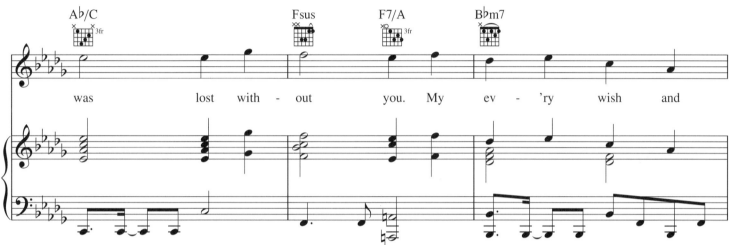

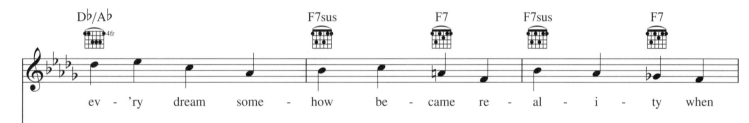

was lost with - out you. My ev - 'ry wish and

ev - 'ry dream some - how be - came re - al - i - ty when

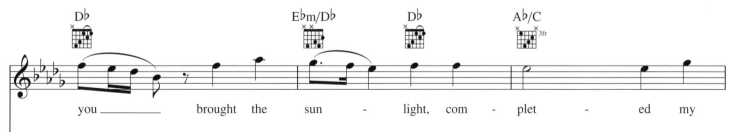

you ___ brought the sun - light, com - plet - ed my

VISION OF LOVE

Words and Music by MARIAH CAREY
and BEN MARGULIES

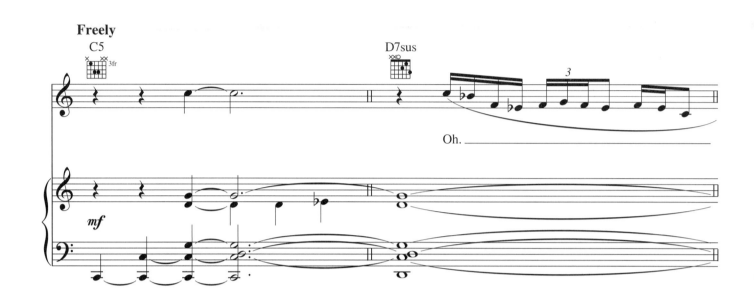

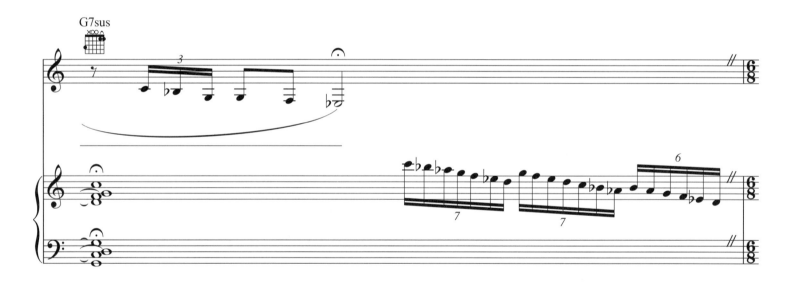

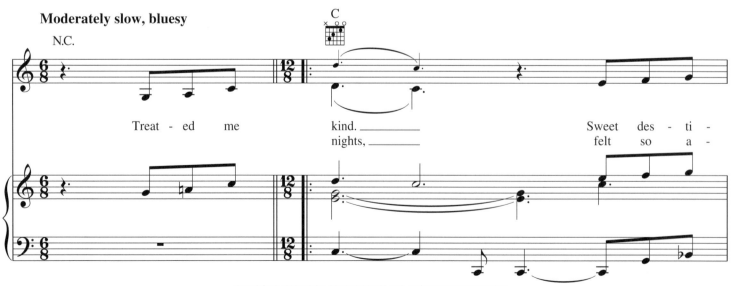

ny _____ car - ried me through des - per - a - tion _____
lone. _____ Suf - fered from a - li - en - a - tion, _____

to the one that was wait - ing for me. ____ It took so long, _____
car - ried the weight on my own. _____ Had to be ____ strong, _____

still I be - lieved _____ some - how the one that I need - ed
so ____ I be - lieved, _____ and now I know I've suc - ceed - ed

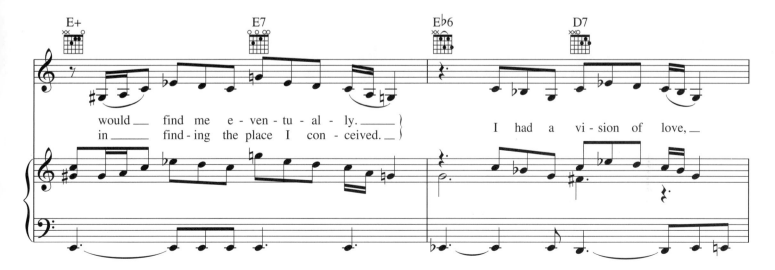

would ___ find me e - ven - tu - al - ly. _____ }
in _____ find - ing the place I con - ceived. ___ }
I had a vi - sion of love, ___

and it was all that you've giv - en to me. _____

Prayed through the and it was all that you've giv - en to

me. _____ I had a vi - sion of love, _____ and it was all that you've giv - en me.

I've re - al - ized _____ a dream, _____ mm, _____

and I vis-u-al-ized _____ the love that came _ to be. _____

Feel ___ so a-live. ___ I'm so thank-ful that I've re-ceived ___ the

an-swer that heav-en ___ has sent down _ to me. You treat-ed me

kind, _____ s-weet des-ti-ny, _____ yes, _____

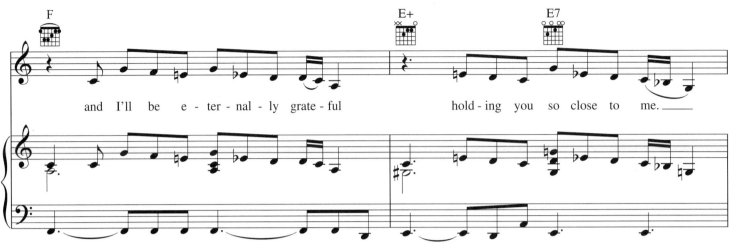

and I'll be e - ter - nal - ly grate - ful   hold - ing you so close to me. ___

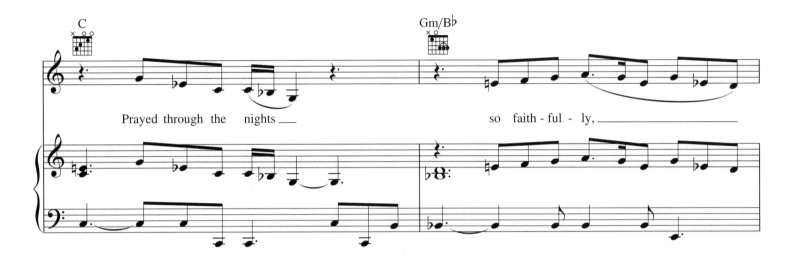

Prayed through the   nights ___   so faith - ful - ly, _____

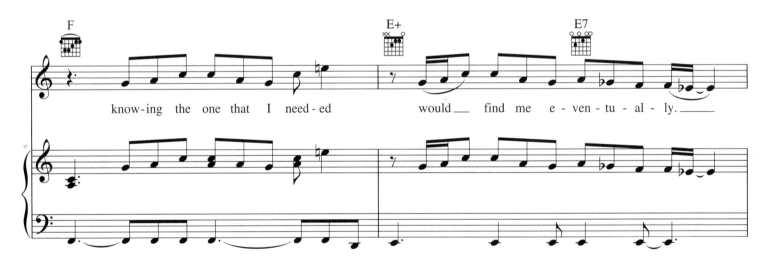

know - ing the one that I need - ed   would ___ find me e - ven - tu - al - ly. ___

I had a vi - sion of love, ___   and it was all that you've giv - en to

WITHOUT YOU

Written by PETER HAM
and TOM EVANS

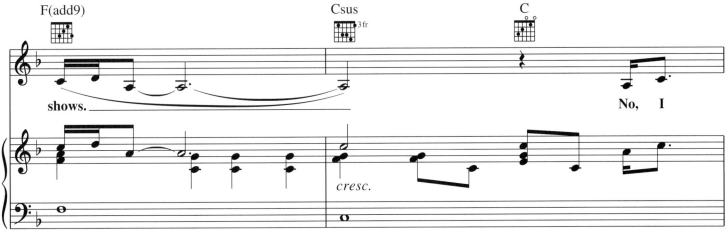

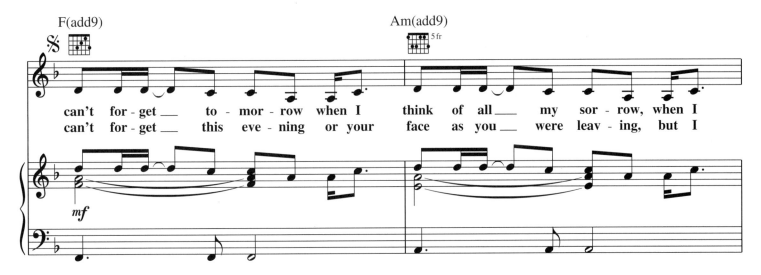

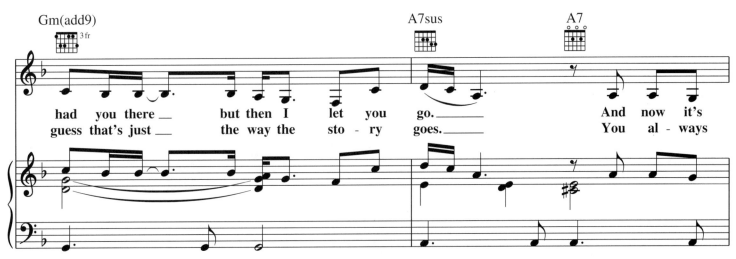

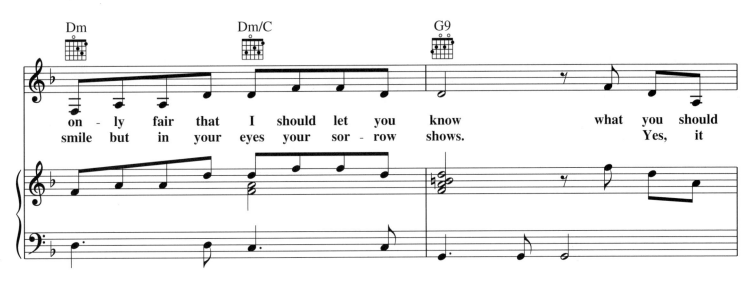

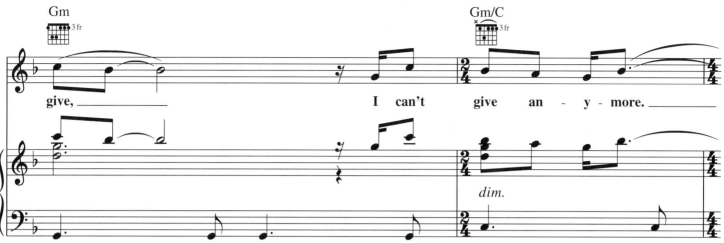

give, _____ I can't give an - y - more. _____

D.S. al Coda

Well, I

CODA

I can't

live _____ if liv - ing is with-out you. _____ I can't

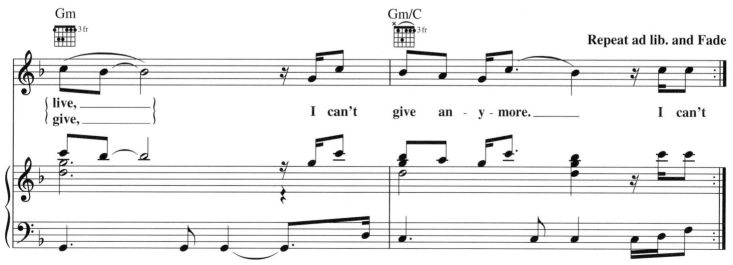

Repeat ad lib. and Fade

live, _____
give, _____

I can't give an - y - more. _____ I can't

WHEN YOU BELIEVE
(From THE PRINCE OF EGYPT)

Words and Music by STEPHEN SCHWARTZ
with Additional Music by BABYFACE

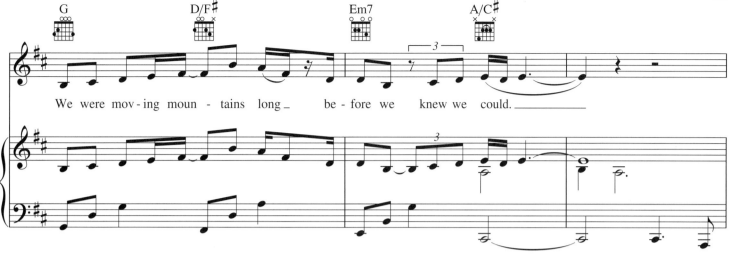

We were mov-ing moun - tains long _ be - fore we knew we could. _____

There can be mir - a - cles, _ when you be - lieve. ____ Though hope is frail, it's

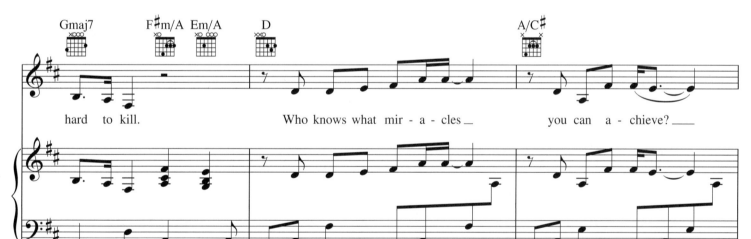

hard to kill. Who knows what mir - a - cles _ you can a - chieve? ____

When you be - lieve, some - how you will. You will when _ you _ be - lieve. _

In this time of fear, when

prayer so of-ten proves in vain, hope seems like the sum-mer birds, too

swift-ly flown a-way. Yet now I'm stand-ing here, my

heart so full I can't ex-plain, seek-ing faith and speak-ing words I

now you will. You will when you be - lieve. _____

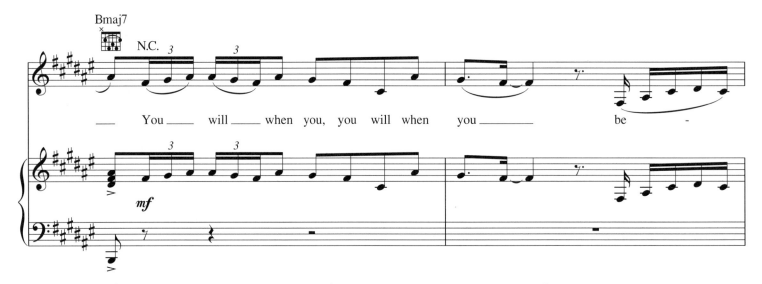

_____ You _____ will _____ when you, you will when you _____ be -

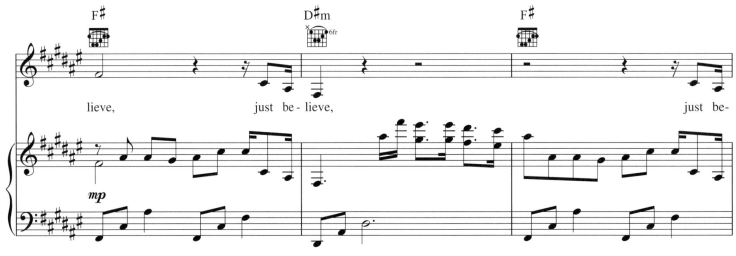

lieve, just be - lieve, just be-

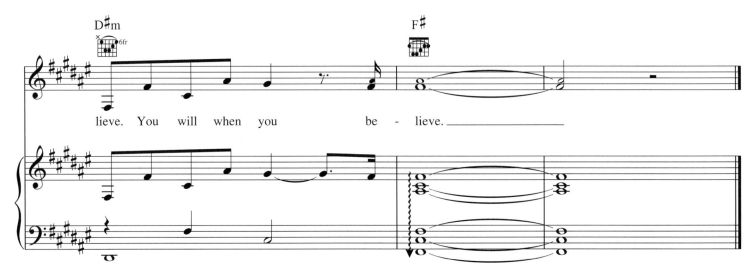

lieve. You will when you be - lieve. _____